EMOTIONAL INTELLIGENCE AT WORK

BUSINESS, PEOPLE & STRATEGY FOR THE MODERN WORLD

PARASHAR PANDYA

Dedicated to the loving memory of my paternal uncle Bhavbhooti M. Pandya. Until we meet again my friend. Thank you for all the life lessons.

Contents

Preface

It is quite naive and simplistic to operate from a viewpoint called things will continue to be the way they are and we can maintain a status quo. No you cannot. However emotive you may feel about it, business is bound to alter in a dynamic marketplace fueled by technology and the human desire for novelty.

The only thing consistent in business is change. And the only thing you gotta keep on doing over and over again is to keep altering the design of your business model. Reinventing oneself is nature's way. That is how God meant the world to be.

As change is permanent so is the opportunity to change and alter to stay relevant. It is a constant battle between man's fundamental tendency to remain in a state of inertia and man's profound love for the new and variety.

A paradox is what man is ultimately. My work experience of over 17 Years in the express and logistics industry and interactions with the finest minds in corporate India gives me a unique perspective. I call this perspective the 'eyes of an outsider.' Looking at one industry from the eyes of another.

People shape the culture at the level of organization. The question is then what shapes the individual? I am yet to meet a human who isn't seeking success, peace and happiness. And very rarely have I met people not wanting success so their emotions are pacified. This is massively insane actually. But it's true.

The first place to start is to ask why we get sentimental in the first place. We will begin by examining how we are wired as a species in how we respond or react to external stimuli.

Then comes in language and how it forms and shapes our life experiences. Do animals get emotional? Of course, they do? Does that impact their performance? Million-dollar question. In fact, two people may have a completely diverse response to the same stimuli, thereby bringing forth a different set of results.

As an entrepreneur you have a critical role to play, being emotionally intelligent and maintaining sanity at the workplace is sacrosanct. You hire people, form teams and lead the people. Ultimately what needs to be managed is everybody being on the same page.

There are lessons to learn and mistakes to avoid from our friends bygone. Also there is success to be celebrated by those who dared to alter and reinvent their businesses. And then there is Steve Jobs who says, I want to put a ding in the universe. I wish you the best and a rocking success in your professional journey. Bon Voyage

ACKNOWLEDGEMENTS

I thank myself for believing in me at all times. My wife, without her support and care I couldn't have held it together. It's just the two of us, life is a blessing together.

I

How technology has altered our world forever

I remember vividly watching the first Nokia advertisement on TV with curiosity and who can forget the tagline. Nokia - connecting people.

The Finnish giant captured the imagination of the world and ventured into a previously uncharted territory. For the next decade Nokia ruled the hearts and minds of people and crucially the market with complete Monopoly, the unspoken word in business.

My first phone was a Nokia 3310 and showed off my work commitments and importance with awe and gasp to everybody in college in 1999. Alas, those were the days.

Following this giant leap in technology came the first phone and obviously from Nokia with a camera and Bluetooth technology. You had to have it and you had to be boisterous about owning it.

When my father bought the first Motorola home, it was untouchable. He placed it on the table. And we could only see it and the pride and arrogance lit eyes of his. When traveling out of town he would place it in the cupboard locker at home for many days in a row. I know it is unthinkable for the Apple and Samsung generation but you should get that these were the days of 6 Rs per minute on an incoming call and 18 Rs outgoing.

For most people of my generation Nokia was the last word in technology. We spent hours playing the egg eating Snake game and had college and group champions claiming thousands of points and rank. It was the PUBG of my generation.

Steve Jobs was out and very publicly out from Apple and it followed years of stagnancy in the technological world.

Microsoft was the sole owner of the computer domain. Megabyte computers, a small firm, had the first few personal computers with bulky floppy disks as I was enchanted with the possibilities of first hand contact with it. This was in 1996 at Rajkot in Gujarat, India.

Computers continued to be black and white and boring with a dull screen and dim background light. Data was the name of a magical new word we all learnt and MS-DOS was like OMG the next gen space technology.

You didn't really have a childhood if you didn't have a cardboard model of the personal computer with a fake mouse.

The first personal computer we bought cost 85,000 Rs. Yes you read that right.

Then suddenly the skies shattered and the winds blew and the earth moved. Steve Jobs was back at Apple and a whole new era of computers and mobile phones unveiled themselves.

So now, Apple PC was the most desirable piece to own, Microsoft lost its sheen and Nokia was almost over the edge.

I had a new phone with camera and Bluetooth and a radio and a TOUCHSCREEN. Yes, I was the king of the world. That was my first taste of the predecessor of Android. You had a toothpick stick to use the phone with. It was the new sexy thing to do.

The most unforgettable presentation was made by Jobs launching and announcing to the world the arrival of the Apple iPhone. This was followed by Samsung launching a Touch screen phone with the Android system.

Blackberry was the new tool of the tech savvy corporate MBA grad.

Nokia had its days numbered now. Android ripped apart the major stake of the phone market mainly eating into the share of Nokia. Apple however was the Mercedes of the expensive phone owners.

Blackberry had an interesting albeit downward spiral journey too. It was unique in terms of its software and exclusive system and closed loop apps. They made hay while the sunshine lasted.

The process of transformation is quick and painful. It used to be slow and lengthy is a thing of the past. Look how fast the world changed and the growth and perish of some of the biggies happened.

Within decades Yahoo, Google and Facebook achieved gigantic growth and scale and a massive customer base. Compare this with the industrial giants of the last century.

Kodak sounds like dinosaurs, so prehistoric in terms of its irrelevance I am not even going to mention the name again.

Microsoft bought Nokia and tried breathing it with a new life. Tried, because it didn't really shape up as envisaged and is sadly not even the shadow of its once glorious past.

Technology is just one of themany industries wheremany giants died a slow and painful death. The retail sector or brick and mortar were another such biggie.

The farmers and small time manufacturers found their godfather in a new class of business owners, the Retail shop owners.

Throughout England and America and the African continent a new generation of business owners came up with the idea of taking farm and industrial produce to the masses. The retail sector was born. And more than 200 years later many of them proudly recognize themselves as retailers. You will find old lanes and streets in many parts of the world with shops in operation for more than 100 years.

The retail merchant purchased goodies at dirt cheap rates and sold the stuff to the retail client at 100 or 200 percent margin. It was the golden age of trading.

The media and art reflects contemporary society and its moods. If you read the books like Merchant of Venice you would find the harsh massive wealth and powers of the retailer and the muscles he flexed. This stayed the same to the end of the 20th century and beyond. If you were rich and powerful in a Hindi or an Indian potboiler you must be a wealthy merchant. Gold and Diamond smuggling was a rich profession and respectable enough even for those with a criminal bent of mind.

Some store owners took pride in the fact they do not have any other branch and they do not home deliver and have no discounts to offer.

Then came the style or fashion or practice of having multiple branches in the same city mostly in the old and new market and even different cities. Some even went ahead and spread wings across the country.

The concept of brands and bags and labels and the affiliation of a brand ambassador was perhaps the first from the retail segment. Magazines and newspapers carrying black and white or color images of the superstars of the yesteryears are still etched in the memory of a lot of oldies.

Retail brick and mortar stores kept growing and prospering while the farmers and manufacturers suffered in silence.

This continued well into the late 90's until Amazon happened to the retail sector. Amazon dramatically altered and reshaped and damaged and dramatized and screwed the retail sector and the middleman like an atom bomb. In fact shop owners had their a**es bombed back to the Stone Age and camel ridden deserts of the 70s.

There are undoubtedly millions of stores worldwide and they continue to remain in operation today as we speak. But they lost something very crucial. The profit margin and the blind faith of the consumer, forever.

I could buy a laptop off the internet and have it shipped from a warehouse in Hong Kong to my apartment in Leicestershire in the UK at a much cheaper price than the local computer store. The year was 2004. Imagine the impact and state of affairs today.

A very crucial next chapter will actually elaborate on what exactly Amazon did and then others followed suit. It's a major case study for an inter-industrial impact and seen from the eyes of an outsider revolutionized business and particularly the retail sector to eternity.

But what led to the demise of these enterprises? What was the poison that acted as a killing agent? The dinosaur vanished from the surface of the earth, once perhaps the largest and the most powerful animal on the planet. Let's take a look from the perspective of the consumer: what killed the Goliath? Kodak (I know, I know I said I will not name it), Nokia, Blackberry, etc. Just how did the curtain fall?

For the consumer for a long time the purchasing power existed only on paper. In reality they were at the mercy of the giants. There are distinct non things that make life miserable for the common man. Product quality that alters the life of an individual and the service that makes one feel valued and appreciated.

In the absence of interest in serving products and services empathetic to human needs, the giant expects the consumer to be a bot, non-human that cannot question what is doled out to them.

The only and only factor that keeps a business alive and kicking is the consumer. If the consumer loses its game , No matter how big you are or how much money you have or the political clout you possess.

The business must evolve with the needs of the consumer.

We were not just happy with the telephone therefore we got a cordless phone or a car phone. We were not just happy with that so we got a hand phone or cellular phone. We were not just happy with that, we wanted a still and video camera too. And we got what we wanted. From someone or the other. And whoever served. Won. So many companies and thousands of people at large organizations with particular skillets are no longer desired.

Does anybody remember the pager? We wanted to be able to reply. So we got the SMS or text messaging. We now have Whatsapp and messenger and we can send files and pictures and videos too.

The personal computer was too bulky. We wanted it everywhere, so we got a laptop. The laptop was eventually too heavy and we got the tablet or iPad. We now have the computer on our mobile phone.

I am the consumer and you cannot take me for granted. How I feel about your service and the emotional state you leave me with matters a lot. It's the determining factor between you and your competitor.

As a service provider the telephone company failed to serve me. Made me visit and follow up for a telephone instrument and connection. It was a wedding celebration at my house when the installation was finally complete. And no you didn't immediately activate the line, it took about 15 days. In the 60's the only house in the Khar Bandra locality with a telephone was ours. Your failure to serve caused you to be rendered useless and irrelevant.

If you were fortunate enough to be able to buy a camera congratulations you are the king of the world. Clicking pictures and checking the reel for the number of clicks left had its own adventure. And when you are done with it there begins the long cycle of pain.

You visit a photo studio and handover your personal film to a complete stranger and be given a receipt to come back and collect your pictures with negatives. Undeniably it had its fair share of fun, excitement and joy. But then again it was a process and an exercise.

It was a proud possession of the film reel camera and we have preserved one that belongs to my great grandfather.

Where it failed the consumer was the quality and clarity of pictures and the faulty service of getting the pictures for the family album.

Digital camera was seen as a tentative fade and that's laughable. The audacity to think that you are invincible.

It rendered a whole industry empty and without any meaningful employment.

Digital cameras did away with the need to carry a film around or even trying to find one. All you have to do is use a USB drive and print the pictures or share online.

It was however really the mobile phone that made a 360 degree difference to the way we experience the world.

Let's begin with the basics. When was the last time you bought an alarm clock? Now consider this alright, that for the generation before you it was unimaginable not to have one or more alarm clocks per household. Not anymore. All you gotta do is set an alarm on your phone.

People like my father carried around multiple watches when traveling abroad and some even offered separate dials to have international times be managed. It's absurd today to even think of something like this.

A calculator is the lifeline of a professional or business owner or accountant. In fact every CA or business accounting student carried around one and calculators were given around as gifts. Now by any stretch of imagination I don't see this happening today. In fact it's as if we are referring to prehistoric or ancient times.

The mobile phone camera, god's greatest gift to mankind, especially the ones with a crazy interest in photography. The whole idea of a family dinner or outing with friends or memorable moments with one's paramour is all actions of the times bygone. Every starter, main course, dessert, appetizer must unquestionably be photographed and shared on social media. You may or may not enjoy the food but the world must know. We won't even get into the conversation of selfies. The Less said the better.

The web browser is aptly replaced by the phone browser and email applications on the phone make sure you are always in touch. I stopped using the print newspaper to get my bad news out to the world. I definitely do not have a clear memory of when I used a pen and notebook to write something or take notes. The list is endless; one can go on and on.

I now invite you to glance through a few of the paragraphs above and look at just how many industries or business sectors have been completely wiped out and ended up totally useless and are not seen or heard of. Imagine somebody reading this 100 years from now, it would seem like fiction to them.

This is how technology has and is affecting and shaping the face of humanity. Technology is transforming what it means to be a human being for human beings.

The postal industry or the mail delivery business underwent a massive shift in business operation and its struggle to survive and stay relevant is mythical.

The postman right from the word go was one of the most important person's of his time. If you lived anywhere close to a village or a remote county in the countryside you would most certainly know just how crucial a mailman is. Those who served in a forward area would eagerly await to hear from their loved ones and the messenger was an important man. For most of you today the messenger has a completely different meaning.

Personal letters of love and joy, cheques and demand drafts, payments or wedding invites or information pertaining to the loss of a loved one were all delivered by the postman. Songs and poems have been written praising the man to be doing God's work.

The mobile phone and cellular telephony changed all of the above forever. The advent of the internet and easier modes of communication made the postman a name sake as mostly parcels and legal notices are sent using the mail service today, be it a private courier or government post.

We will dwell upon the express industry and its success later at length.

As it is a clear example of altering the business model to stay relevant and both private and government owned companies in the express and mail industry did a fabulous job of reinventing themselves. The usage of electronic facilities for money transfer and email based bank and other financial statements left little or no need for physically shipping a piece of paper any longer. The express industry had its Who Moved My Cheese moment. And they relocated the cheese elsewhere.

II

Lack of willingness to alter

Blue Dart failed to anticipate the impact of the ecommerce wave. The express delivery business was hampered by internet and online processing of major documents. This also did away with the need to ship physical papers on a priority basis.

The major hit to the Blue Dart business model was it operates India's only cargo airline meant for quick and dedicated cargo movement. Now, the problem is due to eradication of state conditions like Octroi and VAT. Major biggies have their warehouses and road transportation is cheap. What this effectively did was take away the need for same-day or overnight shipping by air.

So this is where we in the express industry were by a sledgehammer. The Dehlivery, Ecom Express and other third party delivery service providers to the ecommerce giants like Amazon and Flipkart work on a hyper-local model. They typically operate like an independent company in a city, as a local entity and not parts of the whole.

Who'd have imagined the hub and spoke model would have a replacement? Hub and spoke was the be all and end all of the express industry. FedEx started with this and Aircrafts carried everything from mail, to milk to newspapers. The world was revolutionized and strongly connected with this system of operation.

A huge hub at Memphis, Texas in the US where hundreds of planes could land and take off was built by FedEx. After segregation, stuff was carried to different parts of the United States. This was adopted as a standard by the world.

This was seen as the present and future of the world. But a little innovation called the internet changed all this and changed it forever. The new hyper local model is not only much faster but also more economical where the standard wait time is less than 24 hours. Indian companies did not see this Tsunami coming. They failed to estimate the extent of damage this change could cause. A lot of regional and domestic express companies were either sold out or shut up for refusing to adapt to this change.

Swiggy and Uber or Big Basket work on a hire for delivery model and that works well such that they can stay low on the manpower costs. It's the monthly running expenses that make or mar a business. And if you can stay light you will do well.

If you are a David do not worry about the size of your business. In fact if it's smaller it's easier to manage and alter and you can be quick at that. You can always micro manage all your processes.

In fact a Goliath like Reliance ADA had a major downfall and loss of business and repute.

This was a classic example of gross mismanagement and lack of foresight into the basics of making a business profitable. As a small or medium enterprise you always have the advantage of being able to manage the minor ship holes to avoid sinking in the long run.

And we will be here again.

III

A New Pair of Eyes

And it still looks just the same. But there's not a doubt about it. Everything has changed - Nicklas Sahl

Eyes of an outsider 1

My work experience in the express industry gave me the privilege and honor of working with people from different strata and business spectrums. I mean who doesn't need or use a courier service? This allows me a unique opportunity to have a distinct view and perspective of the business world at large. I am sure no other business allows such exclusive hobnobbing with the rich and influential and educated simply because they need you. The eyes of an outsider is looking at an industry and its operations from the perspective of your own business model. Your own industry and how it operates differently than the others.

We will discuss at length the process of looking at the manufacturing industry both wholesale and retail from the eyes of an outsider who comes from the express industry. How does the manufacturing industry operate right from the yarn to fabric to production to wholesale to retail? How does the ecommerce boom impact the fashion world? What has the internet changed? The size and scale of it. The competition from China and other countries. Challenges in India. The growth opportunity. The idiosyncrasies and lethargy of the people. The lack of education and exposure. The express industry and how it operates.

Indian cotton and fabric was known to be famous since Roman times. The legislators complained how loads of gold was spent paying for the Indian Muslin Roman women had a taste for. Since the shipping industry was well developed in India at the time fabric was loaded and exported to remote parts of Europe and Africa. Indian cotton export to the African continent continues even today. Fabric merchants travelled along with the goods and sold stuff on the way. These long voyages and adventures are well documented. The glory of Indian made clothing brought British, French, Portuguese and Dutch sailors to Indian shores.

With the Industrial revolution in Europe Indian fabric played a pivotal role in the growth of British and European industries. British territories across Asia participated in the money making of her Majesty's government. These territories outside India would later go on to beat the Indian manufacturers with their quality and pricing. But we will come to this again. Post Independence thanks to the imperial policies the industry was almost on the verge of a collapse and most small-time artisans had shut shop. The Indian government put in efforts to revive the sector.

But what really worked well were the Indian businessmen and their unique entrepreneurial skills. The flourishing mills of the 60's and 70's brought life and business to Mumbai and other industrial cities of the country. The Bollywood potboilers of the time had the hero or his father working for a mill owner. He fights the autocratic system and the moral battle results in a landslide victory for the common man. Indian exports to Europe, US, Africa and Asia kept building up well into the 80's and 90's. The Indian Diaspora world over favored Indian ethnic wear for women. The Western wear market was largely dominated by the Chinese and other Asian manufacturers like Vietnam and Cambodia. The scenario is still the same.

Now, here's how the manufacturing market is currently working in India. The yarn suppliers sell to the fabric mills on credit basis. Note the word credit as it has a long lasting impact on the business. The mills sell in return to the wholesale fabric traders or resellers. They sell fabric to the manufacturers. The credit cycle here is 4 to 6 months. The manufacturers design and sell their goods to wholesale traders of readymade goods. The credit cycle is anywhere between a month to three or even more. The wholesalers sell these goods to the retail store owners. The end consumer buys from the retail store. And this completes the cycle. The retailer is obviously at an undue advantage because they buy in credit and sell cash.

The functioning of the express industry however, is completely different. The logistics industry has different verticals mainly Transporters, couriers, Angadias, etc. The modus operandi is very clear. You have a parcel or shipment or document to be sent from location A to location B. The courier service provider carries the shipment and charges you a sum of money agreed upon for the services rendered. The payment was made in CASH only. You may avail of a credit facility if you have a large transaction on a daily basis and the payment is to be made weekly or fortnightly or monthly. The entire chain in return mainly works on what we call cash and carry basis. Cash and carry is you pay cash and we carry.

The customer decides which company to use primarily based on their speed and efficiency meaning the service record. You CANNOT thrive in the express industry without speed and efficiency. Losing an article for carriage would mean adequately compensating the consumer for their loss incurred.

Let us look at the manufacturing industry from the eyes of the express industry. The malady of the manufacturing industry as a whole in India lies in its lack of speed, efficiency and lethargy. They have no freaking clue of the very values we in the express industry swear, live and die by. Bangladesh, Vietnam, Cambodia, Thailand and definitely China thrive on the lack of these operating values of Indians.

Every person and service provider engaged in the manufacturing industry lacks the value of time. Placing an order means you may or may not get the goods and the delivery is mostly slow and delayed or deferred as we call it. And when the factor of time is lacking or missing most certainly there is no integrity with regards to the payment to be made. Thus starts the never ending cycle of debt and mounting losses. So there you go. No time, no money. Simple.

However, one of the world's largest fashion brands operates quite differently than the rest. They have adopted a perspective and style of operation that is distinct and unheard of in the fashion world. And this is a worldwide phenomenon not just limited to India.

Eyes of an outsider 2

Zara: A case study. Amancio Ortega started Zara in 1975 with a single store in Coruna Spain. Besides Zara he also owns other major international brands that add to the wide range of product repertoire that the Zara group boasts of. More than 200 designers come up with over 10,000 designs each year spoiling customers for choice and all this at an affordable price. Zara has new products in their closely located stores every 10 to 12 days vs. the world standard of 6 to 9 months on an average.

If a certain style or design becomes the new must-have on the street, Zara gets to work. Designers churn out the new styles and they're fast-tracked to stores while the trend is still going strong. Store managers communicate customer feedback on what shoppers like, what they dislike, and what they're looking for. That demand forecasting data is instantly funneled back to Zara's designers, who begin sketching on the spot. Zara also has extra capacity on hand to respond to demand as it develops and changes. For example, it operates typically 4.5 days per week around the clock on full capacity, leaving some flexibility for extra shifts and temporary labor to be added when needed.

This then translates to frequent shipments and higher numbers of customer visits to the stores, creating an environment of shortage and opportunity. Zara's business strategy allows the company to sell more items at full price because of the sense of scarcity and exclusiveness the company exudes. Zara's total cost is minimized because merchandise that is marked down is reduced dramatically as compared to competitors. Fast fashion is the name of their game and with zero expenditure on advertising, Zara's practices are counter intuitive to the industry and that has them win.

Zara's strong distribution network enables the company to deliver goods to its European stores within 24 hours and to its American and Asian outlets in less than 40 hours. To sum up the marketing strategy of Zara it's based on variety, affordability and speed of delivery. To find out what's available at Zara you could either visit their website or a store. You will find new designs every 10 days. So, every time you enter the store you get to see something new and different. The production facility is huge and centralized with distribution all over the world. This allows for a tight control over their quality and finishing as well as a massive cost advantage.

"The secret to Zara's success has been centralization," says Felipe Caro, an associate professor at the University of California at Los Angeles's Anderson School of Management and a business adviser to the company. "They can make decisions in a very coordinated manner." The company often relies heavily on sophisticated fabric sourcing, cutting, and sewing facilities nearer to its design headquarters in Spain.

The wages of these European workers are higher than those of their developing-world counterparts, but the turnaround time is miraculous. Zara stores are mainly around business districts with many street corners that serve as advertising opportunities and ease of accessibility for the customers. Their supply chain model causes intentional stock outs and stores are required to order within strict timelines to have the goods arrive. They encourage having a lot of empty space. They dispatch in small quantities. If you look at the economies of scale all this sounds outright insane and defies logic. But it works.

The New York Times called "Zara Mind-spinningly Supersonic". Zara has been operating in more than 2,200 stores in 96 countries around the world. That's even crazier. In 2012 Zara reported a consolidated sale of US $ 20.7 Billion. Zara makes 85 percent of the full price on its clothes, while the industry average is 60 to 70 percent. Unsold items account for less than 10 percent of its stock, compared with an industry average of 17 to 20 percent.

"Most companies are riddled with penny-wise, pound-foolish decisions to reduce cost; " noted Kasra Ferdows, a professor at Georgetown University's McDonough School of Business in this article on Bloomberg. "Zara understands that if they don't have to discount as much, they can spend money on other things. They can see the benefit of this certainty and rhythm in the supply chain." This is also the reason why Zara can afford the extra labor and shipping costs needed to accommodate and satisfy changes in customer demand. You'll be hard pressed to find any excess inventory or dead stock in a Zara warehouse.

Throughout the supply chain, lean is the word, all the way from raw materials to the finished manufacturings on the shelves. **Source:** https://www.tradegecko.com/blog/zara supply-chainits-secret-to-retail-success

Eyes of an outsider 3

Zara operates like an express delivery company. Their speed and efficiency can give FedEx a run for their money. Let's look at the similarities between Zara and the express industry that are unknown to the fashion apparel world. At the core of any delivery system lies its speed and efficiency. Also a major cost factor for efficient delivery is transportation, unlike others in the fashion industry Zara doesn't shy away from incurring this expense. They spare no expense to make sure their goods reach the stores in the shortest possible time.

Speed: This creates reliability when you maintain consistency over a period of time. People trust you and your word to deliver, because you have done it over and over again. Speed makes you win in that you are way ahead of your competition. When they wake up to the latest trend you already have in store and selling. The production process in any manufacturing unit costs money and has your funds invested in it, funds that you may be paying interest on.

Therefore, the faster you are the more money you are making and more importantly saving on your production process. You pay interest only once a month to the lenders, however you may make money from the same capital twice or thrice in a month. This brings in more cost efficiency. Speed surprises the competition and has them initiate hurried action that is unplanned and that costs more money. So at all times you keep yourself or your product more cost effective and price efficient compared to your competition and still more productive and profitable.

Efficiency: It comes with systematic planning and advanced order placement from the stores to the factory. That's the first time. In turn the warehouse must deliver the packages using an express mode of delivery. Cargo and Transport services are slow and unreliable. Small packages get delivered faster. This makes you efficient. Trying to save on transportation costs puts you at jeopardy. Long term victory comes from being efficient. You would rather have the stock on display in store than rot in the warehouse.

Transportation expense: Most companies try to use cheaper modes of transportation. This leads to a delay in the delivery of goods leading to some of the following issues. There are very high chances of wear and tear and damage to the goods while in transit. You'd rather have the goods in hand than in a transport warehouse. Again, loss or damage would mean insurance company hassles. Zara works in a way that is counter intuitive to the fashion business and its operating logic. They keep the packaging small and use the express delivery model.

They bring in efficiency by delivering way ahead of others and keeping their stores well stocked. New designs invite more visitors and result in more sales. Their pricing is competitive compared to the others in their range. That makes it easier for the sales assistant to convince the consumer to buy and buy more and often. The new age business is set up in a scenario of dynamic technological innovations. Constant changes and challenges to innovate are a part of daily business affairs.

The startup ecosystem is a fail safe for the contemporary techies and can lie cozy in the financial cushion. This is unlike the 2000's where the dot com bust wiped many dreams and annihilated young techpreneurs.

The background is in the 80's and 90's and more so today Asian students traveled to the US, UK, Europe and Canada for education. Those were the golden days of migration. They struggled and migrated and married and had offspring. They made America their new homeland. The disadvantage of any fall back structure did not stop them from working hard and making a mark, or as they say a dent in the Universe.

Today these entrepreneurs and children who are into business and have an Ivy League degree are a social and financial support system for the techpreneurs. A lot of those who returned to India, China, Japan, S Korea, etc head large organizations and are in a key decision making position. The new business owner finds it easy to get an investor because the Indian or Asian Diaspora have a soft corner for people they consider their own.

This depth of pockets makes a significant difference and has an advantage previously unavailable. Not just the oldies, even those who have studied at Harvard or Princeton and find someone who is an alumnus from their alma mater it immediately strikes a chord and they start off on a great note. Getting funding and in big chunks has never been this easy. Riding the wave many young kiddos are making a name in the big bad world of venture capital driven corporate world. The CEO is getting younger and so is the team that he commands. Getting big is no longer the prerogative of a chosen few. It's no longer only the elite or ones born with a silver spoon who may claim their right to the next big enterprise.

In fact the willingness and hunger of next door kids is beating everybody against the wall. Facebook, Tesla, Amazon, Flipkart, Uber, Ola, Swiggy, Food Panda and many more companies are owned or started by people who didn't have a rich daddy or fancy degrees. They are from the middle class or the average working population of the society. Up next we wanna examine what seems to be working for these new age enterprises. Combined with the right technology and trade basics they are growing exponentially.

We will specifically focus on how a business model can be altered and customized to win a dynamic market place scenario. The case study of Zara clearly suggests the success of a novel or creative yet strategic approach in an already existing industry that is traditional in nature.

The purpose of writing this book is to allow an entrepreneur or a start up to examine their business from the 'Eyes of an outsider'. What we are up to is to transform the past based view of doing business. Do away with all the limiting factors and conditioning that tell you it can't or shouldn't be done. Ultimately, it's the survival of the fittest. Shape up or ship out. We begin now. This is why you bought this book.

The future belongs to those who believe in the beauty of their dreams. - Eleanor Roosevelt

The new future 1

So how did Amazon grow to where it is today with turnover of $135 billion? Amazon performs exceptionally efficiently measured against revenue per visitor, which is one of the key measures for any commercial website, whether it's a media site, search engine, social network or a transactional retailer or offers travel or financial services.

Amazon commitment: They are Earth's biggest selection and to be Earth's most customer-centric company. There are many ways to center a business. But in my view, obsessive customer focus is by far the most important.

Amazon strategy: "Relentlessly focus on customer experience by offering our customers low prices, convenience, and a wide selection of merchandise." We can also learn from their approach to digital marketing in Amazon's RACE marketing planning framework:

Reach: Amazon's initial business growth based on a detailed approach to SEO and Ad Words targeting millions of keywords.

Act: Creating clear and simple experiences through testing and learning. Convert: Using personalization to make relevant recommendations and a clear checkout process that many now imitate.

Engage: Their focus on customer experience, "Customer Obsession" as they call it is shown by the way they consistently outperform other retailers.

Amazon business and revenue model CEO Jeff Bezos: We will continue to make investment decisions in light of long-term market leadership considerations rather than short term profitability considerations or short term Wall Street reactions. "We work to earn repeat purchases by providing easy-to-use functionality, fast and reliable fulfillment, timely customer service, feature-rich content, and a trusted transaction environment.

Free shipping offers are used to encourage increase in basket size since customers have to spend over a certain amount to receive free shipping. The level at which free-shipping is set is critical to profitability and Amazon has changed it as competition has changed and for promotional reasons.

Amazon Customers:

Amazon defines what it refers to as three consumer sets customers, seller customers and developer customers. There are over 76 million customer accounts, but just 1.3 million active seller customers. A loyalty program customer is offered is Amazon Prime, a fee based membership program in which members receive free or discounted express shipping.

Competition: Amazon describes the environment for our products and services as 'intensely competitive'.

It views its main current and potential competitors as: 1) Online and offline manufacturers and retailers of products and services;(2) Publishers and producers of digital content;(3) online shopping sites and comparison sites;(4) Ecommerce, advertising and allied businesses;(5) Logistics service providers who act as third party fulfillment agencies to online and offline stores.

It believes the main competitive factors in its market segments include "selection, price, availability, convenience, information, discovery, brand recognition, personalized services, accessibility, customer service, reliability, speed of fulfillment, ease of use, and ability to adapt to changing conditions, as well as our customers' overall experience and trust in transactions with us and facilitated by us on behalf of third-party sellers".

Amazon marketing: Amazon does not reveal much about its marketing approach in its annual reports, but there seems to be a focus on online marketing channels. Amazon Partnership strategy: As Amazon grew, its share price growth enabled partnership or acquisition with a range of companies in different sectors. In most cases, Amazon purchased an equity stake in these partners, so that it would share in their prosperity.

Amazon marketing communications: Their communications strategies are (unsurprisingly) to: 1. Increase customer traffic to our websites 2. Create awareness of our products and services 3. Promote repeat purchases 4. Develop incremental product and service revenue opportunities 5. Strengthen and broaden the Amazon.com brand name.

Source: https://www.smartinsights.com/digital marketingstrategy/online-business revenue-models/ amazon-casestudy/

The new future 2

How Amazon is consistently altering itself to meet the market needs? When the opportunity presents itself you need to show up. If not, you gotta create one for yourself.

We will now analyze just how the whole

Amazon ecosystem operates and how it is dynamic to the needs of their customers. What are key success principles that you can emulate and create a working model for your business? That's the game isn't it? Knowing about Amazon and others is good but what matters are you designing your own personalized ecosystem that fosters growth and progress?

Inclusive growth: From the British East India Company, to the Rothschild family to the Wal-Mart thrived and accelerated their success based on one and one thing only. Exploitation of the masses. And this continues. The ambition to supersede and be the center force of all power looked beyond the basic human values of respect for the life and dignity of another.

Nothing mattered more than being at the source of all power and money. Accumulation and accrual of wealth was the only uniting force and anybody who betrayed this guiding principle would end up being imprisoned and mostly dead. Some of the most powerful and rich families in Europe and the United States have maintained status quo ensuring passing on of wealth and exclusive social recognition. Microsoft, Apple, Google, Facebook, Amazon, Tesla Motors, Uber are some of the world's largest corporations today.

Do you ever hear or would you associate the words exploit or terrorize and beat down with these companies? In fact together they are adding millionaires to the world by the hundreds each year. The distribution of wealth and sharing with people who work with you is the new norm. Not just the employees but also suppliers or independent contractors are mining gold working with these new world corporations. And it isn't the imagination of a utopian world but a sense of equal opportunity for everybody to do well in life.

Whenever we hear a biggie getting listed or getting major funding we find out they are creating new millionaires. Employees with the ESOPs program. Not just in the US or UK but in India as well. This inclusion is positive and has a far reaching positive impact on the minds of people.

Three Laws of Performance, a book on transforming the business to achieve desired results talks about the sharing of company ownership with your team. It is high time Indian companies recognize the value of staff driven companies and the magical results they can achieve. Today even small companies can afford to install and implement a profit sharing model or an ESOPs program for their team.

Source: The Three Laws of Performance by Steve Zaffron
Wealth creation is a team process. It's like when you are in the bathroom shower, it's you and you only. But when you get drenched in the rain water with your friends, there is fun, joy and celebration. \

Invisible leadership: During the 2014 elections in India a wave of emotion and feelings brought about the downfall of government. 2019 is distinct in that the social media and news channels are full of people leading the way clearly stating the leadership they desire. In the good old days of charisma from Kennedy to Clinton personal attributes won. Oh my god look at him he is awesome.

Leadership today in creating greatness where the audience is. It's not your personal charisma and character but the team leading from front that forges victory. In any business, execution lies with the team. And in execution lies the performance. If you have a team that leads and creates its own plans and achieves the measures your task is fulfilled. Steve Jobs said there is no point hiring and then telling them what to do. Let the team bring you victory.

Infosys operated on the principle of having one man per job. A specialist who does his job exceptionally well with little or no interference. And this guy doesn't really know much of anything else. A master marketing person need not be a great financial manager either. That's what you need to distinguish and operate from. It isn't imperative for all your team members to be great at everything.

Let them do exceptionally well what they are great with. As an entrepreneur no matter what the size of your company, if you have to constantly throttle your team or be after them you are probably better off being employed. Your inability to manage people and their performance is bad for business. A great manager or leader doesn't move at all. Or even better he is invisible. Jokers need to be visible and narcissistic men need to be seen, not leaders.

Young graduates from IIMs and IITs taking on key positions in corporate giants are transforming the ways of the corporate world. In a family driven society like India, the financial success of one individual in the family transforms and elevates the quality of life for the entire family and even the neighborhood. A Sunder Pichai fuels the imagination and aspirations of an entire generation and nation.

Leadership is powerful and leadership is inspiring and motivating. Customer orientation: A customer is not at the mercy of your whims and fancies to serve. Your customer keeps you in existence. The very core of a business demands the presence of a customer to thrive and blossom. Had someone said this to the tea and coffee merchants of the 18th and 19th century they would have scoffed or even laughed it out. Their existence meant creating and maintaining dominance by wielding the ruthless power of money.

Hoarding and depriving the common man and harming his survival were the only services reliably on offer. This deprivation and man's weakness for a fake sense of ego and pride lead to worldwide violence and bloodshed. The revolutions be it American or French or Russian that caused widespread upheaval and loss of human dignity.

Competition is the flow of heavenly nectar that the proponents of Capitalism will offer you as a positive way of life. In a free market economy multiple players participate to position themselves in the financial system and make good of the freedom to prosper. This freedom in turn creates a whole new class of cash rich people who go out and spend. This keeps the wheel well oiled. Developing and retaining a customer over a long period of time requires the customer to experience extraordinary quality of service, a well chalked out product and a sense of being acknowledged, validated and appreciated.

The customer is the very reason for the existence of an enterprise. Customer is the god and indeed one who has the customer is god. The thing with both god and customers is you gotta serve them the food that suits their palate or taste. If you look at any top 5 companies today in any sector, they win because their entire focus is on the user experience. As aptly clarified by the case study on Amazon they are winners because they give their customers precisely what the customer desires. Zara doesn't design for aliens or create unwearable fashion. That would mean doom for them. They give people exactly what they want.

There is another angle to look at here. Henry Ford said if I had asked people what they wanted they would have said faster horses. In other words people may or may not be aware of what is possible. May not be aware what can bring forth more comfort and make their life more workable. This is the task of the dreamer, the inventor, the adventurer, the pioneer. You gotta create stuff that goes beyond the everyday imagination of people. Apple or Tesla motors are doing just that.

Now, not all of us may have the ability to alter the future like Steve Jobs. Revolutionize the world with simple acts of offering extraordinary service and beating the expectation of the consumer. A simple act of a job well done and consistently so will result in growth and expansion and prosperity for your team and for yourself. How will I stand out and make life easy for people? A question you wanna ask yourself every morning before you leave home. Businesses don't win by being the cheapest or selling the most numbers or by being the most expensive one either. They win by offering an extraordinary service experience to all their stakeholders. That includes the vendors too. They are your partners in growth.

Network of people and ideas: The first testament talks about the creation of the sun and moon and stars and rivers and plants and animals and then god made man from his own image. Even god found it odd to create man in isolation. The almighty wished for us to live as a community. In the race to fulfill ambitions of power and money man forgot to create a community as god would have wished him to. And therefore he had a fundamental failure in fostering lasting peace and harmony. Wealth and comfort came in at too great a price.

The SUCCESSFUL companies know, understand and appreciate this. When you create a network of vendors or customers it's a win-win situation for all. The rate and velocity of your growth and expansion is unimaginable. It is like compounding interest. You may begin small and with a few numbers but you do it consistently and you realize you have gone beyond all fathomable limits.

Amway is probably one of the best examples of a network generating billions of Dollars in revenue. As we have already seen in the last few illustrations, businesses that are highly invested in building networks are increasingly successful and have a faster pace of growth. Markets respond pretty well to players that work on harmonizing a vast audience.

Whereas the TATAs and Birlas took 100 years or more to get to a reasonable scale of business, a new generation of entrepreneurs are getting there in 5 years or less. Microsoft took 10 to 15 years, Apple did the same, and Facebook did it in 5 years. Tesla and Amazon are humongous and that too at a much faster pace and short span of time.

IV

Individual performance will shape the organizational transformation

Emotional Intelligence

Vijaypat Singhania, is an Indian aviator and industrialist, of the Raymond group, a perfect story of trust and betrayal. "Don't give it today; put it in your will. They will get it after you're dead, they won't be able to put you on the road," he told TOI. This is written from the perspective of the businessman himself and may not be construed at the absolute or whole truth.

So Vijaypat Singhania has an elder son who lives in Singapore. As per his elder son they didn't get along and, on several occasions, experienced being insulted by his father. Sounds familiar aye, no you may be a millionaire you'll still have these problems. One fine day the senior Mr. Singhania decides to hand over the reins of his business to his younger son and move on to being the non-executive chairman of the group. His son however had other plans. Soon he removed his father from the business and family home and denied access to funds. By his own admission Mr. Vijaypat Singhania never imagined he'll have to go to court with a family feud. Why is this relevant here?

This is just one example of how your emotions get the better of you. A decision made in a moment or time of emotion can be very costly. Extraordinarily expensive as it turned out in the case of Mr. Singhania. Notice how you are extra careful in places known to be dangerous for strangers. For one you will try to avoid visiting a risky place and if you absolutely have to you would consider taking a friend along.

Likewise, I am feeling happy and elated. I am more likely to give away generously. Long scientific studies have shown that people consciously choose passion over reason no matter how compelling the evidence is to the contrary. Acting on impulse and not operating from common sense has had people lose many a million if not billions of Dollars. Your cognitive ability will be of little help, unless you consciously do not work on yourself. You will ignore it, look at the stock market or gambling, people risk losing almost everything, operating from an emotion called hope or having an inflated sense of ego. A deep-rooted fear will always take precedence over knowledge.

I hate driving and always try catching a flight, because I'd rather not engage in slogging for no reason and enjoy the comfort of a flight. A lot of people make mistakes that cannot be corrected later, and then regret. People read exactly the same newspaper and come away having very different opinions on the state of affairs around them. If you are in a happy mood, you will have lots of good things to say about your city or locality. And when in a foul mood you will rant off about how inconvenient and crowded the city is.

Nothing has changed in the newspaper in question, all that changes is your interpretation of how things are, which in turn determines your moods and you come up with a biased opinion. Depending on the positive or negative nature of your emotional experience, the outcomes vary. You judge positively and act likewise and improve the quality of your life with positive emotions.

The same applies to negative emotions as well. You act in a way that is counterproductive and destroys your relationships, health, finance, career and more. It is not the incident per se but the outcome is determined by your moods, feelings and emotions. This is because you act in a way that hampers the outcome for you. One off incidents and occurrences also impact moods and outcome thereby. The announcement of a gift, the home team winning a match, a bright sunny day, all of these can impact your mood and actions. Situational moods can also be affected by the presence of a larger context or authority in some cases.

For example, the awareness that you are dealing with a federal body, or hospital and get you to experience emotions and act quite contrary to how you would have reacted at home. Appraisal and positive feedback increase the tendency of an individual to act consistent to the positive experience in the future as well. Negative feedback tends to cause sadness in a person and may lead to passive aggressive or violent behavior in the future. Expression of gratitude and support can lead to positive reinforcement and may be seen as a rewarding behavior without the need for a tangible outcome.

For example, I donate a few books as charity and the kids who receive them express gratitude and show promise of learning when I meet them. This is likely to elicit a similar behavior from me in the future and I don't really need anybody to praise. Same is the case with Alumni donating large sums of money to their Alma Mater. The point being, my brain experiences release of chemicals that make me feel good about myself. This tells me that such behavior does me good and I must continue to be charitable and generous toward people.

We tend to blame others for all the bad and wrong out there in the world. Human beings shrug and detest responsibility. We ascribe all the negative emotions to others and all the good to ourselves. It is our own little survival defense mechanism. All the good out there I am the one who did it and made it happen. For all the bad out there it was the government, my parents, siblings, spouse, colleagues, boss, etc. Sounds familiar, doesn't it? Fear and anger are seen to impact our view on risk drastically.

When fearful you see things as riskier than they actually are and when angry you are foolhardy in your estimation of the risk in front. Either way both the emotions are a danger zone, you need to step back and take no action. An acquaintance once told me, sometimes not doing anything is the best preventive action you can take.

Fearful citizens of the U.S reported a greater risk perception in the aftermath of the 9/11 terrorist attack. They viewed the world as an increasingly dangerous place to live in and suggested low trustworthiness of their neighbors. Angry citizens on the contrary seemed to be satisfied with the response of the security agencies and expressed faith in the government to protect its citizens. The world is not as scary for angry people as it is for people who are fearful. The angry ones however were expecting stern action and swift policy changes to ensure such incidents are not repeated.

Emotions also determine the depth of your thoughts and how you determine the attention needed to handle a situation. When you feel threatened and consider something to be a safety hazard, the decision to be more careful and vigilant. This is your brain's way of trying to protect you.

Remember, the fundamental task of the brain is to survive your physical body. This comes from our days in the jungle, where survival was everything. The problem is your ability to focus and analytical skills deteriorate with a rise in fear quotient, which means you are more likely to falter under stress and especially when fearful. Anger also has you falter on account of relying on mental shortcuts and heuristics. Thinking or cognitive effort is hard-work. The brain will avoid this trouble when operating from anger, the chemicals released prime you for a Martian battle rather than calm calculated war.

It is after all proven scientifically that 'revenge is a dish best served cold.' Happiness is supposed to reassure you and make you more confident. You are secured in the knowledge of life going well and you expect positive results in the future. Sadness has you be less certain and you are insecure about what life has in store for you. You wanna do better when you are happy; you wanna harm more when sad, or upset or angry. Anger supposedly has you act faster and without much thought or planning; which obviously is a sure shot recipe for disaster.

Low level of anxiety gives you a calm and calculative mind and you take actions with ease. Someone who is highly anxious on the other end of the spectrum will operate from fear of loss and is less likely to take risk. With lower levels of anxiety, you are more likely to take on high risk high reward games. Higher levels of anxiety will have you stick to the known and routine.

This is especially true with job and career scenarios. The decision to get into business putting aside the safety of a job is the toughest choice one makes. Your level of anxiety will determine how you actually deal with this. Sadness also impacts how we are likely to value things and ourselves. We undermine ourselves and our ability to do well in life and deserve a raise or profit or promotion.

In fact, a business study revealed that business owners tend to lower the prices of their products when operating from sadness and feeling disgust for themselves and their business. When sad you devalue yourself and life in general. You set goals less worthy of yourself and aim lower. You settle for way below what you are actually capable of. In a surprising result, people when sad tend to be impatient.

You want to make more money here and now and explore shortcuts for the same. This is contrary to the everyday belief that a sad person has lower ambitions and may not be seeking monetary gains. It's quite the opposite and in an unhealthy way. So, if you find yourself losing patience and are seeking prompt results it isn't something to be gleeful about. You aren't acting out of ambition, you are acting of a certain inner sadness that is manifested in the form of wanting short term gains and expecting to have a windfall of some sort.

We act in a way that is consistent with our emotions or inner world. We act to achieve validation for how we feel. We act in a way that makes right what we think life ought to be. For example, when I am sad and clear nobody loves me; I go out of my way to prove myself right.

Well, the fun part is life will show up exactly as you set out for it to be. Remember, you always will win for sure all the games that you play. You always win all the games that you play. If you are playing that I am a sad loser, that's how life shows up. If you are playing that I'm extraordinary and gifted and blessed, that's how life shows up. So, choose wisely.

Emotions like to act in a sociable way as well. Yes, who doesn't love to feel good, including our emotions? Giving away gifts, praising and applause, helping people in need are all acts our emotions carry out and have a good effect. Next time you wanna encourage someone to be more generous and giving, try and appeal to their heart.

Almost always works to first praise the individual, have his brain release happy chemicals and then ask for what you want. Easy, isn't it? Emotions help you understand others better, help you punish or reward certain behavior and invoke desired behavior patterns or the ones similar to yours.

Remember what goes around comes around. When you give out anger, you are inviting some. Individuals who do well at work and socially seem to have found the right balance to use their own emotions and elicit the right ones from others to get their job done. At least as far as a professional career goes emotional intelligence definitely works powerfully.

In the professional realm there are emotions that run at the level of a group. Teams that work together and mingle regularly have an emotional connection and bond that binds them. Although there are definite advantages to this emotional bond, such unity can be counterproductive in the long run. When you spend a lot of time together, start liking each other and emotionally connect (remember it's all chemicals) you are looking for peace and harmony.

Just like a family structure you are avoiding conflicts. But this is not the final purpose of teams at work. You are working to get results, getting something accomplished. Which means straight and not so pleasant conversations and confrontations are necessary. You need to perform and demand performance from your team members. You need to hold each other to account and this can be painful as all confrontations and demands are. Therefore, avoiding giving in to emotions and attachment is a necessity of the business world.

The thing about emotions is they are like a hand grenade or short burst of bubbles. They went away sometime. Time delay is an efficient method of making things real, distant, aloof and cold.

Email is the miraculous doctor at hand that allows this time delay and helps dealing with work issues calmly. Imagine any mail trail that has really been getting on your nerves, consider if you were to have that conversation with all of those people in person. That's right, it would be a nightmare. An angry email sent out is usually responded to by a calculated response stating there would be a 24-48 hours delay. This calms the nerves.

Open and honest communication is priceless. Suppression is a bad move, and proves counterproductive for both the brain and the body in the long run. Suppression often results in deep rooted resentment that keeps popping up in a sort of passive aggressive manner all the time. This can be far more damaging in the long run than a one-off heated confrontation. It is therefore prudent to take a moment, breathe, pick up the phone and resolve it.

Reappraisal is a very good technique with a positive impact on the psyche, thereby giving you more strength to deal with issues at hand. It is nothing but reframing or rephrasing the stimuli in such a manner that it doesn't impact you negatively.

For example, I did not get very good grades in my final exams. I reappraised it to make it easy by saying, it's just an exam. This allows me to respond better by taking another go at it and saying hey, lemme give it another shot. Reappraisal is a far more effective tool than suppression and users do not show any long-term psychopathology.

Emotions can also be counteracted by another emotion in return. This is a dual-emotion technique to get a desired result, although by its very nature it is biased. You are upset with a friend and tell him some not so nice things. At the end of it all, you add something positive like but I really care for you, you are a nice person.

So, rather than getting a negative reaction, you are now enticing the other person to operate from a positive approach. Advertisers use this all the time to get a positive consumer decision. Say I am trying to sell you a computer that is obviously quite expensive compared to others in the market. With all its fine qualities, I also offer you a very heavy discount on the final selling price.

Now, along with the concern that you are buying an expensive product, you tell yourself I am also getting a huge discount. Suddenly the purchase, even if unnecessary, doesn't seem that expensive. At work hard work and effort is often driven by higher incentives for better results. This has employees willing to undergo a crazy amount of stress simply because it seems worth it. You may find working long hours, on holidays and weekends painful.

However, you are made ok with it by the company in terms of the money you stand to make a result of it. Negative emotions can be seldom dealt with by crowding them out. You have a disagreement with a member of the family or a colleague. For the sake of winning the conversation, you offer them a lot of facts and figures to prove your point. This only clouds the situation; there is no real resolution here. You only end up feeling stressed and exhausted at the end of it all. It's always best to deal with the situation at hand.

To summarise, 1. Emotions can influence and hamper the decision-making process, often resulting in unwanted effects. 2. Emotions can impact our thoughts and the content and context of these thoughts. 3. We may act swiftly with rapid change of emotions; these can be mindless and serve no fruitful purpose. 4. We can observe and choose to respond to emotions in a way that is beneficial. 5. Emotionally intelligent people deal with their own and other people's emotions more effectively than the general population.

V

What drives and ticks human beings and individual performance

Emotional Intelligence

How your emotions screw you. Why am I emotional?

Is it relevant to ask this question? The battle of Mahabharata is on; warriors are ferocious, waiting to taste blood. Just as things are getting charged up Arjuna starts with his sob story. O Krishna, my friend, the most compassionate, these are my brethren, my flesh and blood, how can I murder them?

Lord Krishna, was perhaps the world's first performance coach. Without losing a moment, he said, well, it looks like your flesh and blood is up in arms against you and if you don't kill them; they will most certainly kill you. It doesn't seem like they are approaching to give you a big sloppy kiss. What followed was a book-long conversation that I am not getting into here but primarily Lord Krishna clearly admonishes Arjuna for his lack of self-control and unwillingness to act in self interest. To get a detailed insight into the conversation between the two greats please read the Bhagavad Gita in its entirety.

Also, begin to ask yourself a question. The people you consider your own and family, kith and kin, etc. Are they really acting like one? Observe the behaviour of people closest to you and choose how you should be dealing with them. Do they deserve the gift of your generous love? Or are they acting in a way contrary to your expectation of them?

But the problem with human beings is, we must know. Very well then, go on and read up.

Let us understand the brain science and chemistry that drive our emotions, and in effect drive us. You will begin by looking and reflecting on your life. Go back to the earliest memory you have of yourself and your life. Look at where you lived, your family, siblings and neighbors. Where were you brought up, where did you go to school. What color was your school uniform, who was your first school friend? What did you like eating at first and all the different things you tried and the tastes you developed? When was the first time you came across an unpleasant experience? When was the first time you remember crying, feeling rejection, hate, trauma, pain, anger, rage etc.?

If you look closely there is always a pattern. One thing leads to another and another and another; you came up to be the person you are today as a function of your responses and life decisions made early on. The purpose of engaging in this exercise is for you to stop and give thought to how you shaped up your life and a moment of different response or action could have meant a completely different tangent for you.

When you are in this state of flowing consciousness, watching your life like a movie reel played backwards, you have an opportunity to practice being still. Stillness allows you develop a sense of stability in the head that is critical for extraordinary performance on the outside.

The ability to stay calm when all else around is falling away, and you clench your victory on the edge of the cliff. I mean come to think of it, who are you or who am I except the life choices and actions derived from a set of emotions that we seem to experience as humans. You meet and engage with a lot of people on this journey, loving, learning and fighting, drifting apart, getting close, becoming a completely different being than when you started.

This is really an inquiry into who we are as human beings and really confronting ourselves, before we even start talking about the brain science and chemistry behind it. Because what will matter is how alive and kicking you are to see your life in the new realm of what you are about to discover. Any action you take consequently will greatly impact the real chance of beginning to cause a personal transformation.

The wiring of the brain and the chemistry of our emotions:

The brain is wired to survive the human body and maintain sanity; this is an anthropological phenomenon, or historically over a period of centuries the human species has had to survive overcoming grave natural hardships. So, there are senses, there are perceptions, feelings, emotions and then there are thoughts.

We have hundreds of inputs coming at us every single moment, and our brain determines what we want to focus on in the present, and if it weren't for this discretion you would end up what we call in layman parlance a mad person or be crazy.

For example, as you read you are unaware of the feeling of the socks against your feet. Now as I say you start to sense the same and become aware of it. Basically, you have a sense and your focus on it makes you aware or present to the sense.

Feeling, by the way, is a physiological experience, a perception when your body has a sensation of something; you call that perception of a physical experience a feeling. For example, when you sense a knot in the stomach, shivering of your legs and numbness of your thumb or throbbing in your head, these are physiological experiences that you now label as feeling. The feeling is associated with a particular life experience or occurrence and tagged in our nerves as a memory. Every time you experience a sensation, label it as a feeling, it is stored as a memory.

Now, depending on the outcome of an event you think of it as a positive or negative emotion. It is ironic when you become aware that all the emotions, feelings, sensations, drama, love, happiness, joy, tragedy, anger, rage, so on and so forth are nothing but a chemical process or imbalance in your head.

As a Zen Koan goes, life is empty and meaningless, and it is empty and meaningless, that it is empty and meaningless. All there is, is this and nothing. Everything that you thought meant something, and stood for something and defines you or your life, means nothing. All there is, is your interpretation of a chemical biological process. That's it.

Let's further deep dive into the chemical side of things.

There are over 50 neurotransmitters and your brain releases them depending on the sensation, the memory, feeling associated with a certain experience. We will discuss Dopamine as it is quite well known and usually associated with a sense of victory and achievement. Dopamine release happens when you achieve something, a fulfillment, a victory or success.

So, this emotion of pride and joy that you experience and call happiness is nothing but a chemical release. In that sense we are all dopes, each of us. So much for your stand against drug abuse.

Post Dopamine release, there is an increased level of Serotonin and Oxytocin is produced; this chemical reaction is the scientific explanation of what we call Love. Yup, love is nothing but a chain of events in your brain and you think you are in love.

So, what we associate with the feeling of love is nothing but a nerve memory locked with a particular set of experiences and we think we love this person. All is not lost because the brain fortunately has plasticity, and yes you can create new neural patterns. The key words are focus, practice, habit and mindfulness and we will come to this later. Brain plasticity in simple terms means you can redesign your brain.

Most importantly human beings are capable of having a focused thought. You and I can decide what to think about. You do not always have to lose yourself in a state of flowing consciousness watching Netflix. You are capable of deciding to uninstall an application and start reading scientific journals. So, there is light at the end of the tunnel.

However, all of us experience, perceive and define love distinctly. Why so? It all depends on your story of what you have decided love is and love is not. Having been brought up by parents who are super moral and righteous, punishment for disobedience my experience of love has always been painful. If you really love me, you will let me be. That is love for me. What is love for you?

Take a few minutes at this point and bring your story of love to the foreground. Are humans the only emotional beings, do animals have emotions? Contemporary scientific research seems to suggest that animals indeed do have emotions and feel all the joy and agony as you and I do. How does it matter?

How we act and respond to life distinguishes us from animals. I very often tell my friends, have you ever seen an animal grumble and crib over how life is not fair? Absurd right, obviously not, animals do not whine and moan.

The question is why? Well, because animals can't. Animals do not have language. Human beings have language. Language gives us the ability to verbalize our perceptions, senses, feelings, emotions and thoughts. What a blessing and how blatantly we misuse this gift from our creator.

To answer the question, why am I emotional? You have the ability to communicate your senses through language, to stretch it further, language gives us behavior, we behave from how and what we speak. Language shapes our behavior.

The role of language in creating our experiences

There are over 7000 spoken languages in the world. Language is what separates us from other mammals and animals. We use language to communicate and express ourselves. But a constant question has been if language defines how we think and create how we experience the world outside. Research at language labs seems to hint towards the affirmative.

Now, the problem here is that most of published research in the field of psychology and linguistics comes from grads and undergrads from North American universities and the spoken and written language for most part is English. The problem is the majority of the world population is excluded. Consider the little nuances in a language that makes it unique from the other. An aboriginal tribe in Australia doesn't have a concept of left and right. Everything is defined with directions.

For example, if I wanted to say the cup is to the right side of the saucer, I would say the cup is to the North East of the saucer. The concept of defining things as masculine and feminine is quite common in many languages. The word bridge is feminine in German and masculine in Hindi. So, while a German would think of the bridge as beautiful and elegant, a Hindi speaker would attribute qualities like strong and sturdy to it. Colors are well defined in Russian compared to English.

For example, there are different names for the color Blue in Russian. How does this matter or impact our brain function? Research suggests that a Russian would identify the different shades of a color more easily and quickly compared to an English speaker, because in his brain there are different names attributed to different shades of a color. Our perception of an occurrence is defined by language.

Two people observing the same event will have a different testimony to what exactly happened. In Hindi it would sound insane to say 'I broke my leg' as we say in English, unless you are trying to suggest that you actually broke your leg.

Language also directs and guides on how to treat others and defines the boundaries of relationships. In Hindi a person older than you and younger are addressed differently. This essentially tells us to behave in a respectful manner and is primed. You don't need to be told to speak to someone elderly with reverence and digression would mean disrespect. This distinction is clearly missing in English.

How does language impact our perception and emotions? We will continue with the case for Love. Look at the romantic novels or classics like Jane Eyre or Pride and Prejudice.

In the English language you fall in love. I have fallen in love a million times. I miss you. To tell you in French that I am missing you I would say, 'you are missing from me.' Here almost implying that you are within me or a part of who I am. Now that's some deep love aye. In Hindi you don't fall in Love, love shows up between two people, love is expressed between two people. But no, you never fall in love. Love is seen as a growth phenomenon, meant to take you higher, almost a spiritual experience.

Romantic advances in a Hindi film versus an English one would be different in that there no sexual innuendos in the former. In fact expressing physical interest at the outset would be offensive. Now, this may not necessarily be correct factually and is probably driven by bias, but that's not our subject matter at this time.

Language sets in place rules not just at an individual but a societal level as well. Throughout our written history, from time to time it has meant different things to be a good person, a good human being.

Right now, being a good person seems to mean, studying and getting a degree and a good job. So you gotta start earning and buy a nice house and a car and get married. You now have a pretty wife and two kids. You must take them on a Holiday and dedicate personal time and attention to them. This is the rule. And you are a good person.

Emotions drive our actions and behavior as well. The chemistry of emotions is that you sense a bodily experience depending on the emotion you focus on. My wife yells at me and I focus on the pain of it and that drives stress and the release of chemicals in the body further strengthens the negativity in my mind. Likewise, when my wife praises me I am suddenly on a chemical drive given by a happy sense and experience joy and pleasure. This further elevates my performance in all the areas of my life.

From the paragraphs above science seems to suggest that rather than emotions driving you, you are actually driving the emotions for yourself. Rather than being a recipient or being at the residual effect of and impact of your emotions, you are the one creating and giving out and emanating the emotional experiences for yourself.

The premise is therefore, that you are the creator of joy and happiness and pain as well. Life is not what is happening to you but life is what you are doing for yourself. It is the interpretation of what you sense and perceive that you then define as a particular emotion is what creates your life experience. The whole point being, your life is the way you say it is. So if you are miserable, if you say so. If you say you are happy, if you say so.

The power of language is phenomenal, all empowering. I can think for myself, and make another person think of something merely by using certain words.

For example, imagine having a vanilla ice-cream with hot chocolate sauce over a walnut brownie. It is served in a crystal quarter plate, and you can feel the warmth as you touch it. You can sense that it is freshly baked, and the texture feels just enough to tickle your tongue. Right now, you can actually taste it can't you?

Am I screwed for good?

Two short stories

The story of this guy is a fairytale kind. Shimon Hayut made such infamy that he has a Netflix series based on him. His modus operandi was to act as the son of a rich diamond merchant, woo and wine women in a private jet that he actually had. Now the lady in question is definitely going gaga over his expensive watches, the feel of a soft Armani suit was irresistible.

Now, understand this, what is he doing? First he catches your attention, wins your trust, showers you with affection and gifts, you think you are in love, and Shimon loves you. As you will realize and perhaps already know when high on the rush of emotion causing neurotransmitters, judgment gets hazy. You always make bad decisions when very happy and feeling great, worse than when you are actually upset.

So your prince charming has a problem, enemies of his father are trying to kill him, his money is stuck and he has nobody to trust. Except he has you to get him out of this situation and then you can both live happily ever after. Someone who owns a private jet worth millions needs 25000 Euros. This happens a couple of times and now you are 200 thousand short. He finally writes you a check and that's the last you'll ever see him.

In dozens of countries in Europe Mr. Hayut was wanted and the law enforcement agencies did catch up with him. Actually, two of his former girlfriends got together and helped the police find him. This may be an extreme example I agree, but how many times have you lent out to people you think are family, friends, brothers? More than the money, watch out for people in terms of their actions and how they are only around as long as you are beneficial to them.

A long time ago a village was plagued by hungry monkeys. They would charge into the village with their ravenous appetite and steal all the farmers' lovely fresh fruit and vegetables. Each time the villagers would chase the monkeys away but each day they would return.

Then one day, a wise farmer from another village arrived. The villagers told of their plight and the visiting farmer suggested a solution. 'Cut a hole in a coconut, just big enough for a monkey's hand, and place a juicy banana inside. Because the monkey will not want to let go of the prized banana, he will not be able to extract his hand and will be caught. All you need to do is to pick up the monkey and the coconut and take them to another forest away from other villagers. Within a week the villagers had caught and relocated all the greedy monkeys and peace and harmony returned to their land.

Guess who's the monkey in the story here? That's right. It's the person reading this. The monkey is holding on to the juicy Banana real tight, and the worst part is neither can the monkey eat the Banana nor can he set himself free because he won't give up holding on to the Banana. It is insane right?

Now, let's get you started on your insane behavior. To put it in perspective, begin by examining all the areas of your life.

Look at your relationship with family and friends, at work, your professional life or career, your health and vitality, hobbies, etc. List down all the specific life areas and the current set of circumstances you may be dealing with. Next, pick an area of life that is not working or not working as well as you would like it to. Now consider that in this non-working area of your life, there is a certain juicy banana that you are holding on to.

Think of all those things that make you feel throttled, where you find there is lack of power and freedom or self-expression. That is the price you pay for holding on to the juicy banana.

Let's make it more real, add some flesh and blood to it. Your relationship with your father sucks. You think your father has been nasty with you. You do not deserve a parent like him. You have decided not to talk to your dad to avoid arguments and disagreements. You avoid having discussions with him that lead to heated exchanges. Life goes on and you don't really bother much about it. You have labeled it as a generation gap and that's how it is with others too. It's normal and natural. There is nothing wrong with that.

Now, the problem is every time there is a social gathering, and you confront your dad things get awkward between you guys. There may be occasions where you see your friends and cousins with their dads and you suddenly realize you do not have that camaraderie.

As you grow older and have kids of your own, they want to have a grandpa too like other kids. But they don't have one. Guess what? It's because you are the monkey holding on to the juicy banana called my father is a nasty jerk. The lack of love and friendship, his absence in your life and that of your child's is the price you are paying. The lack of freedom in having a father figure, especially when he is alive and can be around can be frustrating. The monkey wants to hold on to the juicy banana and misses out all the fun and joy of life. We will deal with this, but really let it sink in first.

We need to deep dive further and get to the source of this problem that you have. I want to give you an opportunity to look at another juicy banana that a lot of you have been holding on to for a long time, and one of the major causes of cardiovascular and health issues in the world. Consider you are overweight or have put-on a lot of flab over a long period of time.

In medical terms you are an obese person. And this obesity is causing havoc in your life. So, what's the juice here? I mean the price you say is quite clear. There is a definite loss of health and vitality, sexual vigor and agility. This leads to lower productivity at work and impacts your bank balance directly.

Not to mention the poor self-image you have and the medical expenses you incur and the likely hospitalization bills you will accumulate over a period of time. You really are an unhappy fuck, aren't you? But what is even more surprising is the fact that despite all this you continue to be obese and you continue to lead the life style you do? Any normal sane person would act on it immediately right, this is insane. Yet a large part of the world population chooses to live with lack of health and fitness, lack of a positive self-image.

The juicy banana you are holding on to and this is my view, it may be different things for different people, you are ok with your obesity and weight issues. You are ok to have your partner fantasize being with someone else who is certainly more attractive than you are physically. Human beings adjust and learn to give up and relegate themselves to their conditions and circumstances. You are dead and insensitive and are not agitated by the idea of the loathsome person you have become, even if just physically. You are a pig that's happy with the muddy water and the stench and dirt and filth.

In real terms there is not much of a difference between you and a commercial sex worker. At some level you are ok with the way your body and mind are violated. You have come to terms with and COMPROMISED. You are simply lazy and not willing to undergo the pain and agony of transformation. And it is painful as is the case with all transformation. You have learnt to live with your state of inertia. You are comfortable; your comfort is your juicy banana. You are not willing to be uncomfortable. You are not willing to pick up your heavy self and get it to walk and run and jog and gym.

I hope you can fathom the depth of and the degree to which you are unwilling to give up the juicy banana.

In monetary terms you pay extra for almost everything. You are a cost, an additional liability that comes with the extra kilos. I am doing my best to make you wanna jump off the cliff, like really FEEL, insulted and agitated. And I truly pray I am doing a good job with you right now. Coz if you do not realize the gravity and the magnitude of the size of your problems, literally, life will continue to be a living hell for you. Regret is unbearably difficult to live with.

So, when you come to the very end of this existence the realization will dawn upon you, that you had a choice. You chose ill health and obesity simply because it was EASY. The time to make that choice is right now. Honor your word to yourself and commitment to a great life, or honor your emotions. That's what it ultimately is. I would be ok if you stopped reading the book, only if you can get this for yourself.

Your emotions have no bearing on your actions. You chose deliberately, consciously, willingly not to act. You determined it is not a problem to not have a fixed schedule or a routine that you religiously stick to. This is what all the people you consider SUCCESSFUL do. They have the discipline to see through the actions they have decided are going to bring them health and vitality.

So, you can feel sorry for yourself and enjoy the filth that you are in right now, or pick up your ass and get to work. As we move forward you will read and know how you can take charge of your emotions, and these are nothing but chemical reactions as you now know.

You can create, plan and live a life independent of what your emotional world is up to. A life you live in a way that you design it and are committed to. You chose to give up your juicy banana and you now have freedom.

Also please find comfort in the fact that it isn't really as gigantic a task as it seems. There is nothing elephantine about it. The guy next door does it, and so can you. And for sure you have known people who did it, simply because they got alive, and realized being dead is no longer an option. You can decide to live too. And the best time to start is right now!

VI

Your role as a business owner

Emotional Intelligence in action

How people in command of their emotions view the world differently and therefore act in a way that serves their interest. From time to time you come across people who seem to be leading a life of peace, joy and freedom. They are untouched, unaffected and have this invisible protective layer.

And this idea is rubbish. There is nothing extraordinary. A wise man, learned soul, etc. are just people who have realized the futility of emotions. When I say futile, I mean no disrespect to how you may feel for or about something, may be someone.

What I intend for you to get and what most human beings fail to recognise is that your emotional world cannot and does not alter anything in the physical domain. To give a crude yet simple example, if I wanna hit you, I cannot do so merely by thinking or speaking even for that matter. I actually need to use my hand to cause you any physical harm.

Now I know, hold on to your horses, we aren't there just yet. To distinguish your sentimental insanity, I am gonna build on further on my learnings from the Bhagavad Gita. It has always appealed to me as a guiding force, especially when it comes to dealing with my inner self. Now beware, no matter what your religion or spiritual leanings, read this from the perspective of creating value.

Arjuna when facing the Kauravas in the battlefield of Kurukshetra was overwhelmed with emotion and grief. For him it was tantamount to treachery and murder to be killing his own flesh and blood. And of course, maybe if he hadn't, Lord Krishna wouldn't have had the opportunity to distinguish this human weakness for him.

To put it plainly, you have a job, a role, you are duty bound to act in a particular way. Your job is to carry out what you are supposed to independent of what your emotional values are.

In the present world day to day scenario, you may not be faced with such extreme circumstances of having to kill your own brethren. However, the learnings from Bhagavad Gita are clear that human beings haven't really evolved much in the past thousand years.

You are supposed to be up at 7, out of bed and clean and wash and exercise. You need to say your daily prayers, help your spouse in the kitchen, before getting to work. This is a routine, may be boring for you. But it's a way of life.

Now, the alarm goes off and you have a difficult choice between getting off the bed or honoring your emotion, and going back to sleep. The question is very simple, will you honor your commitment or will you honor your emotion called laziness that says hey, sleep some more?

What you choose to do here will determine the outcome of your day. We fail to recognize the impact a small decision has on our entire day and life ultimately. Being up late by an hour will mean you will rush to the office without lunch, no tea and no quality time with the family and no prayers or exercise. You start off by catching up and all you do is to catch up throughout the day. You will eat out, spend more money and ingest unhealthy food. Given that you started late, a lot of chores for the day remain incomplete.

You now have another catching up day tomorrow, and before you realize it's a vicious cycle.

I know you probably think I am trying to scare you by exaggerating but if you look at the cost of honoring one stupid emotion, it is indeed quite scary. If you ask somebody who's retired from active work and listen to their life story, you will know they spent 20 years catching up.

What's at play here is the rule of compounding. No this is not a financial intelligence class, but compounding works exactly the same for human life as it does for money. I read somewhere that it takes 90 days to form a habit with practice. It's a matter of what you are practicing and therefore what habits are you forming. You compile 20 years of emotional stupidity and you have a life full of mess in all aspects.

Your relationships are almost zilch, you are obese, spend a lot of money on meds, the bank balance is diminishing. All you have is a truck load full of stress and a doomed tomorrow to look forward to. As we already learnt, your emotions program the brain to release certain neurotransmitters or chemicals that impact your psycho-physiological functions. And given that this has a fallout effect on every life area, your work and career are crucially hit. In the current context of what it means to be human, financial success plays an important role. Therefore, managing your emotions smartly will define the quality of your life.

Emotional intelligence is nothing but the awareness of your mental and emotional states.

With this awareness comes the smartness to not be given by them and simply focus on the task at hand. Big deal, I already know all this. Congratulations on joining the gang. Not one person, who is dealing with an emotional life issue, is unaware of the fact that you need to take charge of your emotions and not be given by them.

The question is how. Have you heard of the phrase, fake it till you make it? Let me tell you something interesting about your brain. It can be fooled; now don't go tell it OK. This is a secret. The brain lacks the ability to distinguish between physical reality and thought imagery. Put another way, whether you are actually in a car riding on the highway, or watching a film with the same scene, or sitting on the sofa and imagining yourself in the car, all the three are the same for the brain.

Remember many pages ago you learnt that the brain has plasticity. And you must be wondering how it makes any difference. Start connecting the dots now. What emotionally intelligent people do is they are in command of their emotions. And how they do this is by telling their brain what they are feeling. I tell my brain that I am extraordinary and am doing great. It releases happy chemicals and keeps me refreshed.

I am clear on what I want and focus on whatever it is that I intend to do. When I do this, I get to practice being in command of my emotional world. When I practice emotional intelligence every day and focus on what I am up to, I am actually able to create a new neural pathway. Brain has plasticity and therefore I can redesign what I want to sense, feel, think, perceive and experience.

Again, a lot of you who have an overfed head full of positive thinking and motivation can already sense excitement in the air. No, I am not talking about placebo. The self help industry has harmed more people and businesses than it has helped.

What you need to realize and appreciate is the exact correlation between thinking and acting. Positive thinking and motivation are again emotional traps. The key missing component here is action.

It takes cognitive effort, strategy, planning and action to accomplish this goal of operating free from the impact of emotions. This is clearly missing when you are in the audience, listening to a tall, huge, bulky guy shout at the top of his voice. That is insane. When you attend an event like that the only person who actually gets rich is the guy shouting. Because even a phony conversation is an action and takes effort. He decided to make lots of money, planned the event, sold the tickets and is in front of you performing.

So how you design a new neural path is by acting in a way that is contradictory to your old ways of living. It is painful and it is difficult and your brain and body will resist at first. But when you do it consistently nevertheless eventually it will work out for you. And yeah, when the rubber meets the road, you know what you really made of.

I have some exercises for you right at the end to support practice operating from your commitments rather than moods, feelings and emotions. But really what is the key determinant or factor that really helps one take charge of life.

If you can go back to your gully cricket days, all the dust and dirt, noise and patchy wicket. You are out batting and the bowler has just made a run up. You are figuring out where to hit the ball without breaking a window pane. The bowl is bowled and the bat has made contact and off she goes out of the park, hitting a fruit vendor's cart. You know the bowler, you know where he lives, and you know his bowling speed.

Now imagine out of nowhere you have Brett Lee or Shoaib Akhtar come out to bowl to you. I mean the ball is still hard; you aren't wearing any slippers, any helmet or guard of course. The scenario has suddenly changed. The ball is coming at you at over 100 miles per hour. What is going on in your head right now? For me it would be, what if I duck, will it still hit my back or shall I run dropping the bat on the ground?

The ball seemed like you could hit it when your friend was bowling. But when a world-renowned bowler came up the same ball seemed like a hand grenade.

If Sachin or Dhoni had the same bowler coming, it would be a regular day in the office for them. A hook or pull or helicopter out of the park. What's the difference? You just haven't practiced enough. The ball is the same, the speed is different no doubt, but so what? Your response changes depending on the way you perceive the ball to be. This change in perception is a function of practice.

A quick very simple analogy would be, you are walking on the street and kids light up some crackers. You shiver as you hear the loud boom, a chilly feeling running down your body. An army sniper is expected to hunt, aim and shoot a target smack in the middle of a lot of boom. What's the difference? You just haven't practiced. It's a reflex action for a sniper. It's the same with bat and ball. They call it muscle memory in science labs.

A driver in the armed forces drives for 18 hours straight without a nap for months, but it's peace time, why? So, it becomes second nature to you. Shooters practice thousands of rounds every month. The reason is the same, you build muscle memory, and you practice. I clock in about 10 to 12 Kilometers every day. Walking to my mind is the best exercise, brisk walk. And I have been doing so for over a decade now.

When you do something over and over again, over a long period of time, it becomes second nature to you. Without the slightest realization or even evident effort you can continue to engage in any given activity.

For once if I am required to walk, say, 15 or 20 Kilometers, do you reckon that'd be a problem for me?

Similarly, for someone who drinks hard liquor every day, a weekend full of beer won't knock him out. Morality is a human linguistic construct. The brain is strictly neutral.

The brain doesn't recognize the difference between good, bad and ugly. The brain only knows practice. You will get and be what you practice. There isn't such a thing as positive thinking. It's a heap of crap the self-help industry is dishing out like crazy. Your brain recognizes thoughts, daily practices and habits you form over a period of time. No positive or negative charge here.

Man's search for meaning makes an emphatic statement, a rather convincing one on the importance of choosing one's emotions.

In the interest of brevity, it is a book written by a holocaust survivor and his experiences in a Nazi camp. Although at a broader level there are many conflicting arguments made by the author, we will stick to what's of interest to us. No matter what life throws at you, how you choose to respond is what makes a difference. It's as simple as that. Your response is determined by how a situation occurs for you.

Remember, the high-speed cricket ball? Imagine surviving a Nazi concerns camp. And you think you have a tough boss and a selfish family? In a concentration camp, one was stripped, shaved from head to toe, made to work all day with a watery soup or porridge to survive. You ate only enough only to survive the next day and work some more. Now unless you were born in some war torn African state or a third world country, you most certainly didn't see any of this happen to yourself or your family. So, stop feeling sorry for your horrendous life, it's just the way you make it.

An Oscar winning movie Life Is Beautiful, a good film by the way, makes a very strong argument for focusing on the ultimate goal or purpose. It's more of a fake until you make it actually. So, the plot is a family is moved to a concentration camp, the father and son are together, separated from the mother. The father creates the whole thing as a game for his son, making him believe it's a challenge and every activity earns them a brownie point. The ultimate goal for the father is life and freedom, especially for his son.

Man's search for meaning, also talks about a perspective of gaming for life. Consider everything you are doing is a part of the game called life. You have goals and ambitions whatever it is that you are aiming for. All your daily struggles are a part and parcel of you achieving whatever it is you set out to. People you find admirable in terms of their ability to deal with stress practice this quality. The focus is always on the final outcome and objective. The brain plays along, emotions are designed for success, thoughts and habits are in sync. You can make your life mean whatever you choose to.

As Elon Musk said it perfectly in an interview "it doesn't matter whether I am motivated or enthusiastic or not. I just focus on what I am up to." That's the whole idea. Right from Gautam Buddha to pot smoking, Elon Musk means to say 'Get over it'. Being given by your emotions has a real time impact that lasts a lifetime.

Two short stories will make it clear.

A boy was born in a fairly well-off family, the son. As time went by the parents got into financial hardships because the father was unwell for a really long time and there wasn't a source of income. The elder son took upon himself to earn a living for the family. He would earn and spend it all on the household. The idea of saving or investing never occurred to him as it doesn't to most poor or middle-class citizens in a society.

He was extremely emotional about his family and spent it as an emotional decision without giving thought to the future needs or unforeseen eventualities. Years went by, he started and built a fairly large business, making loads of money, way more than he had imagined.

But guess what, he still wasn't saving or investing, it was all emotion for him. The only lesson he had learnt in his head was to earn money to make a living for the family and that is all that mattered. No doubt he had his own personal expenses too. As he started growing old and the children moved away especially due to some difference of opinion, business suffered and the cash flow took a hard blow. Life had returned to the same place where he had started on ground zero. The next story is not very different either.

A girl was born in a large family with lots of siblings. Parents were too busy attending to the guests and relatives all the time. She was trained to cook well and feed well and take care of the household. Feeding people well was all she learnt and knew and mastered. For her blood is all that matters. You cannot falter if you are my blood and I will hold on to you. This was her idea of life.

She moved into business as a matter of financial necessity. But her lack of financial intelligence came in. All she knew all her life was to cook and feed people. She has practiced this for such a long time in her mind that is who she is. Trying to support the family and siblings who weren't up to it and managing business got a frustrating problem for her. Ultimately, she ended up in debts and financial constraints.

Now, if this sounds like the story of your life, welcome. You were born into a certain reality and a reality you grew up with. You continued to practice it for years and now that's who you are. So, I am gonna repeat again, the brain has plasticity and you become what you do over and over again.

Imagine you were born in a fairly well-off family. The childhood was middle class and with age finances improved as well. By the time you are in college the family has multiple cars and you are leading a comfortable time in a Western suburb in Mumbai. With the passage of time, you have a rift with the folks and suddenly out you go. No money, no capital or investments to bank upon. What do you do? Instead of living on a few hundred dollars a month, you are suddenly living on a few hundred Indian Rupees suddenly. People don't wanna have anything to do with you, friends maintain a careful distance. No place to live, no work, no family. What do you do?

Most people would begin with substance abuse, blame the folks, live in the glory of the past and damage their lives beyond repair. End of story. I could, however, write it differently. The only place I always stand in is, what's next and what can I do about it? Life will be what life will be. You have a choice. The choice is very simple. You can choose to act and respond to life in a way that causes miracles. Or you may choose a crib and complain and cry over spilled milk.

Focusing on what's next and what can I do about it gives me a unique perspective to life. I am in command and on the driving seat of my life. Notice there is no conversation of emotion here. There is no feeling or mood to handle. That's the easiest thing to do. It is the most simplistic solution to dealing with whatever it is that you are up to.

You wanna lose weight, run, walk, go to the gym, and exercise whatever. You wanna be healthy, eat healthy and sleep well. You wanna make more money, focus on your actions that will allow you to make more money. The only and only access to performance in life is action. You can have any result for yourself or your life if you operate from an empowering context and act. Simply acting upon whatever it is that you want to alter, will allow you peace and freedom. Life is joy.

Accomplishing as simple a task as finishing this book did not happen overnight. It was a consistent set of actions, thinking and writing and thinking and writing and repeating. There is no emotion to operate from here.

"How Strange, Well, back to work..." These were the words of Elon Musk when Bloomberg announced him to be the richest man in the world. No drama, no story, no conversation, the statement succinctly describes the point I am trying to drive across.

Managing your emotional world intelligently is the best strategy at the workplace and in life. "Work like hell. I mean you just have to put in 80-to-100-hour weeks every week. This improves the chances of success. If others are putting in 40-hour workweeks and you're putting in 100- hour workweeks, then even if you're doing the same thing, you know you would achieve it in just 4 months what it takes them a year to accomplish." I don't read emotions, motivation, moods, etc. in the lines above. Do you?

India is a land of gods. We love to worship and have gods in all imaginable forms. There is a god for every natural resource in the ancient Hindu tradition. The Sun, Moon, Water, Ocean, River, Air, Trees, Birds, etc. you name it. In fact, our worshipping zeal even has movie stars have temples dedicated to them. Same is the case with sports and among all the sports there is the god, Cricket.

In my native tongue Gujarati they say, 'You won't even find a stray dog on the street on a sunny Sunday afternoon when India plays Pakistan.' But of course, India wins every time and we rejoice. Well, I usually stay away from emotions, but here my heart is in the right place.

In sports, unlike life, the goal is clear, victory, the results evident, non-gray and easy to measure and observe. The whole point really is this is exactly how you gotta define your life goals actually. Pretty much the way kids play games, they know and are clear it's a game, but they play like their life depends on it. As you grow, somewhere along the way, you think all this is for real. We will not transgress from the issue at hand. You and your emotions are what we are dealing with here.

Now given the goal is crystal clear managing the emotions is much smoother, not easier, but you know what you wanna deal with. With clarity of mind, you look at the barriers in achieving extraordinary performance or victory, not where the opponent is, but where you are.

Rule number 1, you can only deal with who you and where you are coming from and where you stand. There is nothing outside of you. Never focus on things or people or circumstances you anyway can't do anything about. Now, there is the conversation you engage in with yourself or self-talk and the self-appraisal or reminding yourself of who you are and what you can achieve and have achieved in the past.

This is brain science in action and the plasticity of the brain in full view. Ancient Indian philosophers and grammarians believe that language can make suggestions and bring forth or cause action. Yup, thousands of years back we knew powerful self-affirmations, well before the Western authors picked it up from our books. And there is of course a national rage in India with anything foreign. But this one's cent percent Indian.

So, for example, in the statement the sun has set in Sanskrit Arko Stam Gatah, the literal can be quite simple. However, the statement could mean different things to different people, depending on the intention (Tatparya) of the speaker. To a Brahmin his servant could be telling him it is time for the evening prayers or to go to bed. If a lady says the same to her lover, she could be suggesting it is time for them to copulate.

Coming back to the point, suggestions can be powerful and extraordinarily effective in dealing with our mental and emotional states. Self-appraisal plays a critical role in sports. Sports psychologists and sportspersons use this technique effectively and in a specific fashion to ensure the desired results.

For example, a player says 'I am fit because I exercise regularly.' The idea is quite simple, yet clear and may seem profound to some people. You focus on what you want (fitness) , the goal and the actions (exercise) that you need to manage to get there. It is as simple as that. There is no emotion at play here. Keeping the vision for a healthy self-image clear and at the forefront. In sports both the success and failure are clearly evident for everybody to see. There is no fooling around. And given that there is a very public failure, it is absolutely necessary to manage one's mental and emotional states.

Therefore, the self-talk you engage in with yourself and the consequent actions you take matter. They say players who do well over a long career span are mentally tough. You first win in your head, even before you enter the ground, you are clear. You are the winner. With such clarity of mind, you walk out and simply execute what you already know.

Self-talk is the conversation you engage in with yourself expressing who you are for yourself. There isn't anything outside of you. Don't bother figuring it all out at the outset. Operating from a leap of faith and in your own abilities to overcome the challenges is what separates the champions from the losers. The key function self-talk serves here is I am clear; I am the only one responsible. Nobody outside you has any say in the matter of your performance and you are the one in the driving seat. With this clarity you choose the exact nature of the conversation you engage in with yourself.

Suggestion is also an action. People often mistake talking as inaction, but it is indeed action if done correctly. So, when you make suggestions to yourself that allow you particular thoughts, actions and habits, it is an action. When I am talking to myself and suggest that I gotta wake up at 7, go take a walk, have breakfast, exercise, practice a language, work, make calls, connect with people, appreciate my wife, have dinner with friends, all these are actions.

I am propelling myself to do things and act that impacts physical reality in the world. Much like this in sports when the coach gets after you to practice and run and warm up, these suggestions are actions. They cause the sportsperson to act in a way that brings forth extraordinary performance. Therefore, choose your words carefully. Be mindful of what you speak to yourself and about yourself, because guess what, even when nobody's listening your brain is. Your brain always says, yes boss. Whatever it is that you tell the brain, it follows. It's a no questions asked relationship the brain has with your inner self.

You cannot keep emotions out of business. Whenever you are dealing with the human species emotions are bound to show up. In fact, repressing them can be counterproductive.

However, what is critical to distinguish is there is a difference between allowing the emotions to stay versus being given by them. The thing about emotions is they have a direct impact on your cognitive abilities. This can be damaging in business. Operating from a negative mindset obviously messes up the workplace.

And research seems to suggest a positive mindset helps. Now, my problem with this whole idea of positive energy or mindset and motivation is this. What if I am not motivated or the team is feeling low on energy?

Do we have the liberty to not work? What if it's payday and your boss says I don't feel like paying today. Crazy stuff, right? Given that the nature of business and any human interaction is transactional, nobody's gonna let it go unless you are a kid, or moron or an extremely attractive woman. That's the bitter reality of who we are as humans.

Motivation and a positive mindset are good but are not a necessary condition for performance. Your car doesn't need motivation for ignition, there is an inherent engineering design and the car follows that design. With humans there is an absurd idea of thinking I don't need a design.

Well, there is a design and you need to follow it. Nobody is independent of it or free from it; even if you are the president.

The fundamental purpose and integrity of a business lies in making money and profits. The very survival of a business and the workforce rests completely and solely on positive cash flow. Given the game is to make profits, the actions in business to win the game are clear. Where do emotions fit in all of these? Well, they don't actually.

There are two kinds of corporate executives, the ones who grow and the ones who don't. But before going to that let's look at the fundamental principles that govern all human beings. Gravity impacts and affects all bodies. Whether you are Vladimir Putin or Narendra Modi, if you jump off a cliff you will fall down.

Your actions need to be consistent with what you are up-to in life.

Let us consider the analogy of a car. You have an old Maruti or Chevy that you drive to work every day. Engine is rough, rims are bent, wheels are worn out but it still works. Why this car is ok for you is because what you are up to is using the car to get to work. Now imagine if you aspired to win the Formula 1 championship. What a joke right? You are not even close to being allowed to fill an application to participate in the race, forget actually doing it. They won't let you anywhere close to the track with this oldie.

So, what are you up to in your career is what will define how you ought to operate at work and in life. If you wake up at 9 and rush to work without breakfast and brush your way, this is just perfect if you wanna work as a staff support for the rest of your life.

But if you say, notice if YOU say, you aspire to be the CXO of a company, this level of integrity is totally insufficient. Why? If you consider an average of 100 successful people, the first thing that'll strike you about them is discipline and routine. What it takes to be extraordinarily effective and successful so to say requires extreme discipline. Why so? The reason is simple because from when you begin and when you arrive, the gap is huge in terms of time span.

Therefore, it'll take out of this world kind of discipline to accomplish what you set out to. To practice discipline, you gotta be consistently doing something exceedingly well over a long duration. Hence the second requisite for doing well is to have a routine. A routine is nothing but a set of activities you engage in day in and day out for decades. So, it's not just about a few months or even a few years, but 10, 20, 30 years you do the same thing at the same time every single day.

I'd like to add an analogy from war here. General George S Paton would often say, if you cannot get a soldier to wear his belt or tie his shoelaces properly, forget about him killing the enemy in a face-to-face battle or sacrificing himself for the greater good. Little things are a tell-tale sign of your attitude and will most likely be the same in a critical situation as well.

If you are truly serious about amounting to anything worthwhile in your life, discipline is sacrosanct. If not, stop fooling others and above all else yourself. Learn to be ok with the mediocrity that you are.

How can I deal with my emotions differently and therefore act smartly?

At the outset as an infant, you have no sense of ego. There is no personal pronoun I. You have no sense of self as distinct from the world because you have no access to language. Anything that can be defined, which means drawn, has a limit.

In a way when you define something you limit it. Therefore, with language you realise that there is an I where you are. Ultimately you are limited not because you really are but because language tells you so. But this is not the focus of conversation here. What you need to distinguish for yourself is you decide that you are a distinct identity, with a body, you are I.

Most of this stuff sounds right out of a first-year psychology text book. It would probably shock you to know, as it shocked me that Indian texts written thousands of years back, some even before written text came into existence actually discuss the evolution of identity and self and the world and the universe.

Apart from the fact that language limits you as a human being and turns you into a thing. Coz notice everyTHING can be defined because it has a limit. A sofa, chair, lamp, knife, etc. all have a beginning and an end. Things are also fixed and have properties, human beings ascribe such properties to themselves, we call them adjectives or qualities.

So, as you grow older you start defining yourself, have qualities, likes and dislikes, as if it is fixed and real. You start living your life as a thing. This is normal and common right? I mean that's how everybody lives. Without a second thought you and I operate through our lives relating to ourselves as a mere thing. Take a moment, and think, isn't this insane? Start by examining the impact of I on your life.

The life you live losing out on the extraordinary self-expression you are capable of. The superficial nonfunctional relationships you have, the struggle and hard work in making ends meet. In order to protect your true self, that you believe is real, one loses out in a big way. Say a friend or family were to tell you what you are doing is not appropriate. And you are like, what, how dare you say that to me?

The scenario could be repeated at work or elsewhere in life. The point is you miss out the fun and joy of relationships trying to protect me. Operating from this prison actually limits what you can actually achieve in life. This is clearly evident when it comes to a professional career. Stop taking things personally. You are not the center of the universe.

How you define yourself is a limiting and self-defeating belief. You are limitless and can express yourself as such the moment you get that the I that you believe you are is just that a physical manifestation of the extraordinary self you are. When you point to yourself and say I am such and such. What you are pointing at is nothing but a bag of meat and bones. You have a body; you are not your body. Stop saying I am fat, diabetic, sad. You are not any of that, you have a body that has fat, you have diabetes, you have sadness.

The difference is when you have something, against being something you can give it up. So, if you are not your body, identity, ego, emotions, habits, likes and dislikes, and more, this begs the question, who are you? Who am I? This is not a philosophical question. And there is no right answer to this question.

Across centuries different civilizations have attempted to arrive at a conclusion on the existence of self and the definition of who a human being or person is.

The purpose however has always been to allow a person to be extraordinarily effective and perform at their most optimum level.

What you can begin by examining the size of this universe and make a comparison to your so-called I. The universe is ever expanding. The estimate is that the diameter of the universe is 23 trillion light years. The observable universe is however about 93 billion light years. Closer home the galaxy milky way that holds our solar system is 100-200 thousand light years. This galaxy has over 100-400 billion stars and planets. The size of the solar system is about 287.4 billion kilometers. The earth has a diameter of 12000 plus kilometers and has just one moon, there are over 166 moons though.

Ok so you as a human are about a millionth of a speck compared to the size of the universe. You are just a bloody glib in terms of time given how old the universe is. Your entire lifetime is only a jiffy in the larger scheme of things. That's it. Jiffy by the way is one tenth of a second, that's how relevant your entire lifetime is as far as the vastness of the universe goes.

Hope you are now beginning to get the super dope you are on to even crazily believe that your I matters. It's laughable actually, pitiful of us to try and ascribe any importance to our identity.

The question is what do we do? If you've read the two mosquitoes' poem you would know, stuck is stuck. Or as my dear friend Nirmal says, 'ghoda ni naal ma pag bharaya pachi, dhasdaata jaiye tyaare shu karvu eno pustak ma kyaan ullekh hoto nathi.' This roughly translates to, when your leg is stuck trying to ride the horse and you are getting dragged, the book doesn't say what the best course of action at this point is.

The Hindu Way

Ancient Indian texts speak at length about the human self, soul, brain and the mind. For thousands of years sages and authors have tried to decipher the deeper meaning of human existence.

Why are you born, what makes you human, how do your moods, feelings, thoughts, habits, etc. impact your performance and how can you focus on something and be in command of your life? Before diving deep let's get a sense of the basic terms used by Indian scholars in defining self, brain, consciousness, and more.

The personal pronoun I is referred to as Ahamkara or ego. Chitta is our consciousness that keeps us aware, even while we are asleep. The body with different characteristics is the Prakriti. Mann is the mind and Buddhi is intellect or the intelligence we possess. Mann, Buddhi, Chitta and Ahamkara are the four constituents of Antah-karan or our mental edifice.

Now, if you compare this with the western philosophy, there is a collapse in terms of the intellect, consciousness, nature, ego are all defined as a part of the whole. Our brain is what drives us, the body, nature, thoughts, emotions, etc. There is no clarity or distinction. The problem with this definition is, it's way too simplistic.

Everything that makes us human is supposedly stored in the brain, even originates in the brain for that matter. Before I reveal a final parameter at play here, the invisible hand so to say, lemme give you some context through an example. Sit in a quiet room by yourself. Do not use the phone, laptop, or any other electronic device. As you are sitting alone, close your eyes and be with yourself.

Here's what'll happen next. You will start jumping from one thought to another, a state of flowing consciousness, where you drift from one thought to another. Basic stuff from the first-year psychology text. Begin to observe your breathing, the passage of air, in and out through your nostrils. As you watch closely you will notice the flow of blood in your veins and the mild throbbing of your heart as it pumps blood.

Well, this is great. I am noticing or observing all this, sitting in a room, all by myself, what's the point? Who is observing? Rather the more precise question to ask would be who is the observer? Is the observer distinct from you, the self? In the example above, if you were to ask a question, am I the only one here, and you got an answer in affirmative, the question is who answered. Without much ado, let me get to the point.

The Hindu way of life suggests that the self or the Atman is shapeless, formless and timeless. Every birth the soul adorns a new body, the body is the doer and the Atman or soul is the observer. The highest goal of the Atman is to create oneness with the supreme being or the Brahman or God or whatever superpower you believe in.

The body is just a vehicle to attain salvation or Moksha, release from the cycle of birth and death. Some schools of thought suggest that the Atman and Brahman are one, but for the purpose of practical sanity let's maintain that the Atman is the observer, the body is the actor, a vehicle for worldly deeds and the goal is to unite with the Brahman.

The Hindu way of life therefore suggests one to get that you are a soul, the body is just your present form and the very knowledge of the temporality of this worldly physical existence means that all attachment and personal ego is futile and crazy or meaningless. It anyway doesn't mean anything.

Being selfish is good and important to the betterment of mankind.

Selfishness is defined by the Oxford dictionary as the quality or state of being selfish; lack of consideration for other people. Moral science textbooks in school teach us that thinking of you before others is a bad thing to do, immoral or as we say in India 'gandi baat' or a bad thing.

In a democratic set up colored by socialist ideology it is almost criminal to consider and focus on one's own personal self-interest. It is a good and moral thing to be born poor and live a middle-class life and die in poverty. This is the ideal life of a good, nice, decent, moral person. A whole generation of youth was fed and brought up thinking in this manner of living for the good of all.

The problem with this euphoric ideal is it didn't end up being good for anybody. India remained a poor country, of poor people, technologically backward and socially constrained. The few people who decided to be selfish and bad and morally loose made money and got wealthy. This is an ideal set up for an Indian Hindi masala movie.

Plainly speaking, if being above one's own selfish interests was such a good virtuous thing to do, we should have been super rich, everybody living a luxurious comfortable life. That's not how it actually happened. This chosen middle class or lower middle-class way of life didn't quite work out for anyone. All we had is a higher rate of violent crimes and a few and far in between million-dollar scams.

Be willing to consider what I am about to say for a moment, without judging or evaluating it against what you already believe to be true or I stand no chance to make a difference with you, a fairly stupid thing to do, given you got this far reading and have actually paid for the ownership of this book.

Selfishness is a good thing and it not only helps you do well and prosper and be healthy, but also does the same for people around you. So, from an individual to a nation, selfishness can actually support you to do well in life. How so? We are not on the topic of nation building here so let's stick to our own personal transformation.

Let us begin by considering the very act of selfishness, it begins in the head. You think of what it is that you can do that will end up bearing sweet fruits for yourself. For example, rather than bothering yourself with anybody else you start putting in the effort in your work or career, so you can make more money.

Now, the best part about being selfish is since you are not thinking about others, their voice doesn't matter and you are not bothered by what people think or speak of you. Coz remember, you are selfish now and selfish people don't care what others think of them.

How this serves your interest is you are now free of other people's opinion of you. And given that you are not thinking of anybody but yourself, what others say will not have an impact on your moods, feelings and emotions. You are not getting hurt or feeling offended by what others say. There is no emotional drama around somebody saying something to you or about you.

Imagine what freedom and peace of mind is available. Say if I were to ask for 100 dollars. What would you say? You would say Yes if you had it on you and refuse if you didn't, assuming you'd be happy to lend it to me. Same is the case with happiness and love, you can only give what you have.

So, guess what, if you have love and happiness, you can give it freely and if you are miserable that's all you can afford. Clearly being selfish is super important because you can only pour in my cup what you have. Selfishness therefore is perhaps the most misunderstood of human qualities. Yes, I say quality because it's a good place to stand. Wanting something only for yourself and depriving others is not selfish, it's vicious.

Jim Rohn says you are the average of the five people you hangout the most with. So, if you wish to be rich, that's exactly what you gotta give out. Before you begin to think of loving someone or something outside of you, start within.

Give yourself all the love you can, express it by being healthy and taking care of yourself. Grooming and dressing up can do wonders for your self-confidence. Study and learn, create a great career, live a fulfilled life with your loved ones. Yup, this is what I mean by being selfish.

Empirical evidence that supports a greater control over emotions -

Without much ado let me get straight to the point. Your financial and personal success will work to the degree to which you are in command and control of your emotions and emotional world.

Is there empirical evidence to support my statement? Yes, there is and here is a part of the text from one of such studies. And the bottom-line of the study is "being able to implement emotion regulation strategies is closely linked to well-being and financial success." You will have the highest achievable disposable income and socioeconomic status if you can simply keep yourself in check.

One of the most startling outcomes of the research is that knowledge doesn't make a real difference. Your knowledge on how to best deal with life and emotions has little relevance without practical application of the same.

You may not necessarily be an intellectual but if you can simply follow the strategy to regulate your emotional expression you will do fabulously well in life. It's about how well you drive on the road; you don't necessarily have to hold a degree in automobile engineering to do that.

What is required of you is the willingness to be flexible. Flexibility allows you to do things that you may not completely be aware of or agree with for that matter. It doesn't matter if you think it works, if you simply did it that would suffice.

So plainly speaking people like to interact with and do business with people they like and find similar or socially pleasant. You are someone people love talking to chances are you display an emotional sobriety they connect with someone responsible enough to do business with.

While it is extremely difficult to maintain a healthy emotional mindset, an empowering one especially, when you are in a financial breakdown, it is indeed an opportunity to excel at emotional restraint. People tend to blabber crap when they have a lot of cheese.

It's easier to practice restraint when you have nothing. Further, the study found a positive association between emotional regulation and financial success and socioeconomic status. Emotional restraint or control also helps in terms of how you are perceived by the world outside.

This is not to suggest that you gotta be a people pleaser or try to act in a way that people like you. Come to think of it, the harsh reality of life is, your success will depend on the support and faith of how people around perceive you to be.

Whether you are a business owner or politician to a great degree the perception of who you are by an external observer determines whether they vote for you or support your business idea.

Unless you are already Elon Musk, it will help your own personal financial goals a great deal if you are seen as someone who is matured or sorted. The way people are whether you like it or not, I am not going to trust you if I think or see you as a nut job. It would therefore serve you to come across as a sensible and responsible person.

When you come across as a responsible person you are believed more easily to be someone who is competent. That's correct; people assume that you must be competent because it takes a great deal of mental strength to be in command of your emotional world.

"The ability to be perceptively in tune with yourself and your emotions, as well as having sound situational awareness can be a powerful tool for leading a team. The act of knowing, understanding, and responding to emotions, overcoming stress in the moment, and being aware of how your words and actions affect others, is described as emotional intelligence. Emotional intelligence consists of these four attributes: self-awareness, self-management, social awareness, and relationship management."

A Navy Seal veteran, Gleeson is the founder and CEO of TakingPoint Leadership, former Navy SEAL, globally recognized speaker, award-winning entrepreneur and a bestselling author. Here are some of crucial learning's that he shares with a former Navy Seal.

You begin by assessing your own self and your strengths and weaknesses. When you realize the limitations of being human, you have an opportunity to develop some very fine qualities. These are the ability to be compassionate and sympathetic towards others as you get that they are as human as you are.

With this wise learning you can now communicate with people in a way that allows for effectiveness and fosters a healthy long term relationship. You are seen as someone trustworthy, kind and a leader of people, as someone who stands with them.

All of this requires extraordinary emotional restraint, loud speeches and motivational Gyan won't be sufficient to see greater longt erm success. Your ability to stay in command of your emotional self will matter above all. The purpose of sharing this excerpt from an article written by a war veteran is for you to understand that in a war, you are in command or people die. The magnitude and gravity of being in a life and death situation far outweighs our daily domestic issues.

If a soldier can and does, so can you. No big deal. Moreover, individuals who were better able to identify and distinguish among their current feelings achieved higher decision making performance via their enhanced ability to control the possible biases induced by those feelings.

A 2007 study by Seo & Barrett suggests that whether emotions are actually beneficial or harmful to decisions may largely depend upon how people experience, treat, and use their feelings during decision making, but also points to an alternative approach in which both functional and dysfunctional effects of feelings are equally acknowledged and simultaneously managed to maximize their positive effects and minimize their negative effects.

The art of separating the Fuck from Sentiments

The greatest access is to reduce the time spent on responding to an emotional experience and bringing back your focus to what matters the most. Usually, it helps to focus on the task at hand. This can be tricky and takes rigorous practice.

The flow of events is, something happens that interrupts what you are up to, say a friend accuses you wrongly, for no fault of yours. You are in the office working on your laptop, now completely consumed by the harsh words and totally on it. Nobody better mess with you now, especially that annoying colleague or he's had it today! You keep to yourself for the rest of the day, finding an empty spot for the evening coffee. The day ends with a quick pack up and you head home. Kids jump on you with joy and the wife offers some snacks. You are still overpowered by the stupid words from a long-lost friend.

If you read this paragraph again and again about 6-8 times, you will realize how insane this is. But then who we are as humans, this is the way we lead our lives. At some level you may have practiced masking your emotional experience, which is fine, a practical necessity in the modern world, I guess.

However, this will in no way bring release from the shackles of your emotional response. What you want to practice mastering, over a period of time is to get over your emotional responses in a jiffy.

It's very easy to get on it, getting off is the challenge. So, your wife says something, you have a response; you identify it and decide not to respond to it and get off it. This process has to be done in a minute, less than a minute actually. How fast can you move with this, what's your best response time? Mine is about 5-15 minutes, masters can do it within 1/10TH of a second.

The thing is this is like climbing a mountain with no end; you never get on the top. It's a lifelong exercise or endeavor you engage in. Always remember whatever gets measured gets accomplished.

You can write to me at parasharbpandya@gmail.com and I'll add you to my WhatsApp group. Please share your name, profession and phone number. To begin with I have a formula for dealing powerfully with your mental and emotional states and to practice focusing on what matters.

The thing is this though; the only and only thing in the world that can bring forth performance is action.

If you act and practice what you learn you will start seeing the results in about 3 months or 90 days. What you need to do is hold yourself together for 90 days and keep practicing. As an afterthought before we get to the formula and workbook let me leave you with a powerful lesson. The art of mastering emotions requires you to learn not to take anything personally. Nobody can hurt or hit you with their words.

Nothing can cause any damage to yourself as long as you do not allow it to. You must have read or heard this a million times now lemme show you how to do it for real.

Say you use profane words for me, the worst language one could imagine, my response is, got that, thank you very much. So here's my secret trick to not respond to what anybody has to say.

Tell me, when a person abuses you, does it cost you anything? Does it deduct 10 Rs or 1 US$ from your account? Does it lead to loss of business or income or loss in any other substantial manner? So, it's free right? Tell me what in the world can you get for free today, where even water costs money? And here is this fine humane soul, offering you some choice words for free. If you look at the level of vibration it is actually a real thing, that has money value to it.

So effectively when somebody abuses me or gets upset or angry, they are ideally spending time, energy and effort on me. Tell me won't you be grateful and thank a person when they give you something for free? I would be a grateful soul. The idea is to operate from gratitude when somebody offers you something for free. Isn't this crazy powerful?

The average American makes about 53,000 US$ a year, which is about 20 Rs a minute. So, every time somebody spends their effort on you, count it as per this rate, keep a record on the spreadsheet and send them a thank you note with a little something. What a way to win over or piss off? Either way you are the winner.

Here's the What's Next formula

I am gifting it to you, and it's free to use and pass on, share it with your friends and family and help them win. This formula works perfectly well for any life area. To begin with I recommend you pick an area of life that is supercritical and a burning issue that you are committed to alter immediately. Work on it and get it going and then pick another area. After about 3 months, you can start taking on multiple areas at one go.

The What's Next Formula:

1. Area of life you are dealing with that is not working as well as you would like it to: (FOCUS ON THIS) My weight loss / income issues / relationship with my father. (Spell this out as specifically as possible)

2. The emotional experience I have as a result of it not working: (STRIKE IT OUT) Anger / frustration / Sadness /

feeling helpless

3. The actions I will now take to alter this area: WORK ON THIS AND THIS ONLY, THIS LIST IS DYNAMIC, YOU MAY ADD OR 101 EMOTIONAL INTELLIGENCE AT WORK EDIT OR ALTER IT AS NEEDED.

A. Walk everyday

B. Call 10 new prospects everyday

C. Take my father for a movie over the weekend.

Here's the problem, most people stop at point number 2. This is your default response to a non-working life area. You start working on your emotional experience trying to resolve it and feel good about yourself. And once this emotion is resolved I will go on to work on my life area that needs to be working.

I mean this epitome of insanity I have only seen in human beings. Why on earth would you deal with the emotional experience rather than dealing with what's not working? Rather than losing weight you start being ok with being obese. That's an extraordinary move. This is so good. Kick yourself.

Imagine you are standing in front of a mirror in the bedroom. Looking at yourself closely, you see a streak of grey hair on your head. Would you try to color that mirror image and expect your hair color to change? I mean who does that, that's crazy right? Bravo, Eureka you got it. Dealing with your mental and emotional states and expecting to alter or transform your life is just as crazy as the analogy I just shared with you.

You cannot deal with the physical reality out there by dealing with it in your head. You cannot have babies by shagging and you cannot build muscle by imagining yourself in the gym. It takes action.

You NEED to ACT on WHAT you WANT out of YOUR LIFE. The only and only access to performance is action.

So again, let's repeat, Area of life, emotions you have about it, your actions. Of these three what can you alter and manage? Your action, right? That's all you can do. So, make more calls, walk more often, DO more of what you want, Work on the Area you Care about.

Make a list of 10, 20, 30 things you can do to alter the area of life you are committed to transform. Start working on the actions from the list. Strike 1, strike 2, strike 3, strike.... Strike 30. You got it. Don't worry about it, I got a workbook for you in the end, use it. Print it if you like, paste it on a poster on your wall, work from your laptop or phone, what's important is you get the job done, how you do it is irrelevant.

I am writing this chapter sitting on a chair in a hospital with a family member who is admitted, using my phone. You got problems? Guess what, everybody has problems. The most successful and accomplished people have problems. You gotta be ok with having a problem. You gotta be comfortable dealing with shit that life throws at you. This takes practice. Start practicing being ok with things not working or shaping up the way you want them to. Start working to make things work.

Operating business like in relationships and family like in business

Do not assume and create agreements.

Acceptance is the key. Commit quality time. Be authentically interested in people. Honor your commitment. Communicate and respect others. Human beings are strange animals. Yes, you and I are truly weird.

We take the most important people in our lives for granted. Then act shocked and surprised when they act in a way that serves their interest at the time.

The moment you are up to the time you go to bed. Think of all the people and things that they do for you that you take for granted. Who makes you tea or coffee every morning? Who cooks your meal or packs your lunch? Who makes your bed every day or cleans up your mess? Perhaps it's your mom, wife, brother, father or someone close who cares. Ever notice they don't need a reminder or signal to do it for you every day. They just do it.

Now imagine one fine day they don't pack your lunch or leave your bedroom in a mess. You are shocked and amazed, perhaps even upset and pissed over it. Now read the following statement very carefully.

'Your assumption of their agreement to do your chores, is not their agreement, unless they explicitly agree to do it for you.' In short, your assumption is not the other person's agreement. What rubbish is this right?

Who gets an explicit agreement from mom or dad or sister or partner or spouse? Here's an exercise I assure you isn't available on Google or anywhere out there. Unless you read this book I assure you, you haven't seen anything of this sort ever. Do this with someone in life who really matters, someone important.

Take a pen and paper and draw a vertical line right in the middle of it. On the top left write the name of the person you are doing this exercise with.

My wife: Next write the top 5 expectations you have with this person. 1. She will love and care for me. 2. She will cook me some good food. 3. She will support my decisions. 4. She will respect me. 5. She will take good care of the kids.

Make sure your partner does the same with your name on top of their 5 expectations of you.

Next, here's what you're gonna do: exchange the papers, give your paper to your partner and take theirs.

The next part of the exercise is, against each expectation that the partner has written, mark it as agreed or disagreed. Both of you will do this simultaneously. Once done, return the paper to the other person.

Now is the final part of the exercise. Say of all the expectations you have; your partner has agreed to three but refused two. So, what are you gonna do? I mean if it's your wife or girlfriend you'd say I am gonna separate or divorce over this lack of agreement and you could.

But what about your parents or siblings? Can you get a replacement father? How about a brother? This is a dilemma. What do we do now? The answer is pretty simple. You have only two choices, accept them wholeheartedly with all the agreements and disagreements they have with you or choose to move on.

Here's an analogy I wanna leave you with and a choice that you alone can make. Long back we had no car as we couldn't afford one. Then we bought our first car in many years, an ambassador. We were super happy as it was sturdy and spacious and kept us warm. After a few years we realised it was too slow compared to a Maruti on the highway. Later we bought a Tata car, an Indica. But it was a hatchback. We weren't quite satisfied and then we bought a Tata Indigo Sedan. After a few years we realised it costs too much to maintain. Finally, we settled with a Maruti, looks good, fast, low on maintenance, super good mileage. But then it isn't as spacious as some of the other cars, and the story goes on.

I know many people who have a BMW and Mercedes and they aren't happy either.

Moral of the story is every car comes with its set of maintenance issues. You need to understand that's the case with people as well. Every person has some or other behavioural issues that you may not be ok with. You need to learn to live with people despite the differences. Changing people or relationships won't help. You need to change the way you look and perceive. People do things for you without an explicit agreement is a function of their love and generosity. You need to act generous and return the gift.

An average mid-level executive spends between 8 to 10 hours in the office 5 days a week. That's a long time considering you spend about 30 years as a professional or employed person. No wonder you lose track of your wedding anniversary and forget how old your kids are and what school they go to, who their friends are, etc.

But this is indeed the sad reality of the modern world. It is not how long or how often you spend time with your family, it is the quality and focused attention you put in the time you happen to spend with your loved ones. Let us dissect this further. Your spouse and kids understand the financial compulsions you have that keep you away from home for a very long time. That's a given and no denying that. What is critical is how present you are to their world and what's happening around them.

Whether it's the new dress your wife bought, or the football team your husband is cheering or the excellent remarks your child got on the report card; are you fully present and aware at that moment, perhaps not.

There is a simple but effective exercise I learnt during my training at Landmark Worldwide, perhaps the world's finest personal training and development company.

You do this in pairs and there's no pen paper needed. All you gotta do is ask the other person what they had for breakfast. That's it, absurd and too mundane, almost a cliche conversation starter.

Person 1: So, what did you have for breakfast this morning? Person 2: I had a cup of tea and biscuits. Then half ate a sandwich and packed the rest for the office. Person 1: Ok. Cool. Person 2: Thanks. (Wondering what this is about) Clearly there is conversation or dialogue building up here. It's a monotonous routine inquiry.

Now we change the scenario a bit, this other person that you are talking to is a potential client with a million-dollar contract. You're gonna have the same conversation but listen like your life depends on knowing what he or she had for breakfast. It means the world to you to know who they are and where they come from.

Person 1: So, what did you have for breakfast this morning? Person 2: I had a cup of tea and biscuits. Then half ate a sandwich and packed the rest for the office. Person 1: Sounds like you had company this morning. Person 2: Yes, my husband loves to surprise me with all kinds of fancy sandwiches he learns about online. Person 1: Super, your husband seems to be a fun person to be with, not to mention has culinary interests. Person 2: Actually, he is a scientist and spends a lot of time working on offshore projects. In his spare time, he watches all these shows on YouTube that talk about cooking. Person 1: That's fantastic, lucky you. Person 2: (Almost blushing) Thank you. I am fortunate to have him, yes.

What just happened in the text above is a Real Dialogue happened between Two People. You took Authentic Interest in getting to Know the other person's World.

And guess what, that million-dollar contract is 90% yours. The reason is the world is full of interesting people, what the world needs is someone to take Authentic Interest in truly knowing people. From not knowing anything about your customer you suddenly know, they are married, have a great partner, like to explore and are open to new experiences.

Sadly, you could've expressed similar interest in your partner or child, and you don't because they don't bring you a million dollars. The greatest respect you can show someone is by being fully and completely with them when you are talking to them. A lot of people don't like Bill Clinton, the former U.S president, but common people who have met him have reported, when you meet him and he greets you, it almost seems like you are the only person in the world or in the room at that moment.

The same is true for your little promises, that you conveniently forget about. The movies, or shopping, or theme park that you commit at home. What's the problem here, what's the big deal? The problem is the person who gets out of bed, is the same person who goes to work. When you practice something for a very long time, then you become that. We already discussed this at length in the previous chapters.

The impact of these tiny lack of integrities shows up over an extended period of time, not instantly. The trouble is it's more often than not, too late already. You've missed the bus, as they say. As technology reduces physical interaction or one on one interaction, rather than ignoring, it's time we are more particular or attentive to communication and respect people's time and effort when they reach out to us.

Say we are sitting in a coffee shop, face to face. You ask me something or tell me expecting a response. All of a sudden, I turn my face away from you and start looking elsewhere. What sort of an experience am I likely to leave you with? It would be pretty insulting and hurtful, won't it? That's exactly the kind of experience you leave people with when you don't answer their calls or don't call back or don't respond to messages.

Again, this is a major deal breaker. The key is consistency in communication over a long period of time builds credibility and trust. To communicate is the simplest method one can use. But it is a potent and extraordinarily effective way of earning respect and being trusted and liked. All of these are important ingredients in a business and likewise in a personal relationship. The access to having extraordinary relationships is to leave people with an experience of being respected and valued. You want people to know you value and respect their time and therefore they are truly important for you. They matter to you.

Look around, I mean the world struggles and aches for this. The easiest way to succeed is to give people what they most want out of life, and you'll have everything that you want for yourself and your life. The mantra to an emotion free action filled life and peace of mind. Mantra is a Sanskrit word in origin and in layman parlance has the power to impact reality, almost magically. It is the ancient Indian version of abracadabra.

And unlike this meaningless word has a deep life defining value to it. Nevertheless, in the interest of brevity that is extremely dear to me let me spill the beans on this one.

The Mantra I have for an emotional drama free and peaceful life is:

1. This is what is so. Acceptance of who or what is, just the way they are, and most importantly the way they are NOT. Resistance causes friction, friction causes things to repeatedly persist, and persistence causes pain.

2. So what, what's next? Firstly, does it concern and matter to you? Whether a person or situation, does it concern you in any way? Does it really matter? If not, why bother anyway. If it does though then, here's what you wanna fully focus on and dedicate yourself to.

3. What can you do to alter the quality of the situation, or interaction with that important person, and how can you elevate the quality of your life? We are looking for an actionable access in step three.

To sum it up: This is what is so. Now what? Look at what's next. And what can YOU do to alter the quality of your life? My job gives me an income of 2 Lac Rs every month. That's the reality of my bank balance. My current state of affairs doesn't allow me to live the life I intend to or offer the best of what the world has to my family.

What can I do about it since this is extremely important to me? What actions will allow me to alter this? A possible answer could be, I need an additional source of income, a new business may be, side hustle as they call it. How much I got after my regular work hours, how about weekends, what skills I got that can make me more money, where can I save time by cutting off unproductive activities?

A. 3 hours in the evening. B. 24 hours over the weekend. C I can play the piano proficiently / I am a good salesperson D. I can approach European or American companies to sell their software services in India for a commission. Or teach students in the community how to play the piano. E. Uninstall Netflix. F. Create a brochure and start marketing my services online. G. Perhaps set up a small website and an Instagram account or LinkedIn to spread the word faster. Write a blog and share the link on my WhatsApp status. Performance calls for action, there is no space or place for drama.

It's like a coach once told me about sex, if you hot, you are hot, if you are not, you are not. Rest is a story. You are either in action working a plan, or you are not. Rest is a story.

Start walking the path, and the best time to start is right now, and things will eventually fall in place. God knows better, so stop being a wise nut.

One final word about action, and this is a crucial piece of support. Action plans are always dynamic, you are quick in eradicating what doesn't work, and with speed implement and scale up what does. Simply put, don't be a stiff ass.

VII

What is alignment and why does it matter

Think of the time you decided to start your entrepreneurial journey or simply decided to start a business.

As the idea evolved and shaped up in your head you discovered a vision and mission for the business and the journey commenced. After long years of hardwork and effort you now have a team of people working with you, an enterprise.

Like most business owners, here's the challenge for you. How do you get your team to see the vision exactly the way you envisaged it? How do you get the team to see the purpose you are upto fulfilling by running the show? This is perhaps the toughest part of your journey.

Here's the problem, there's nothing wrong with the team. You just haven't invested the necessary time and effort. If I were to ask you, in all honesty, how many hours, days, months, or years did you spend in having a clear picture and pathway for the business? Let's suppose 5 or 10 years?

A fresh graduate or a professional working with you for a few years, is totally ill equipped to get without you explicitly sitting them down and having a tete-a-tete, boy here's what I am upto. I doubt you ever did that. And then you have the audacity to complain of your team's lack of understanding.

Apart from the quality time required to be spent, the more core issue is the timeline that people think they have or they need to bother themselves with. A time frame that one bears in mind when thinking, planning or acting on something. As a business owner or founder, you are worried about how the industry will shape up in the next 10 or 20 years.

The CEO plans to have a roaring next year or at least a bit better than the last. The President hopes he has a great quarter and can earn his perks. The Vice President is waiting for a raise and praying to have a great month or 30 days. When you get down to the level of a trainee or freshly appointed executive, he somehow hopes to survive the day.

Let me show you a visual representation of the same:

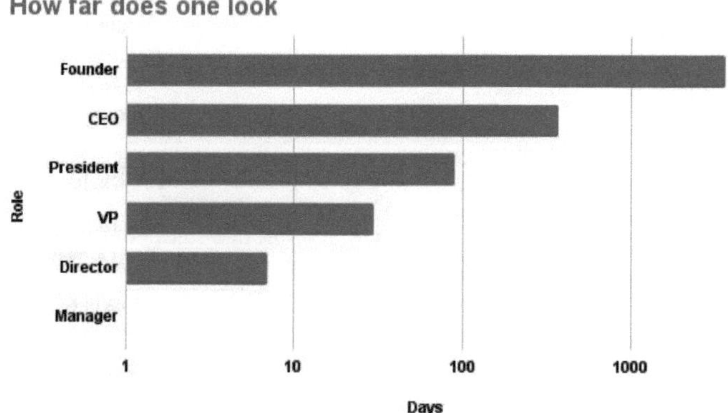

Looking into the future

Now, it's quite clear isnt it? All of us want different things, and have widely different sets of concerns.

No wonder there are such issues of team alignment in my organization, how does one see eye to eye with a person that's looking at things from a very different timeline?

But then as a business owner, you do not have the luxury of things being so simple do you? You want to and have to get people on the same page. The question is how do you do that?

Let us look at what exactly we gain as an outcome of the job we do. A founder, CEO, Manager, or Executive, all of us get paid to do our job. The singular outcome is we make a certain sum of money consistent with the value we bring to the table.

And what is it that you do with the money? Look at the graphical below:

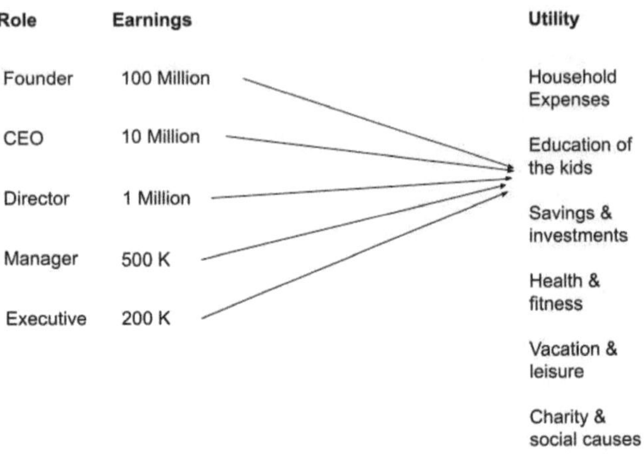

Disbursal of income

As you can see, depending on your earnings and the available cash for spending, the founder and the executive have pretty much the same set of expenses.

The problem is that of clarity and articulation. The simple and the obvious often go unnoticed, and in business and in life, ignorance isn't exactly bliss. What is required is to bring forth clarity that everybody and everyone on the team is playing on the same side. And we are all in this for one and only one thing, fulfilling our personal and familial needs. So what's the fight all about?

In the absence of this clarity and a well defined vision that is both easy to understand and follow with definite sets of actions, there is bound to be friction and mishaps as we have all experienced. I've always believed that the soft skills are actually the hard stuff, technical skills can be taught, learned, copied, etc but the behavioral aspect of work is the toughest to crack and handle.

To make it worse, the HR or the L&D team today functions like housekeeping. Ever visit a coffee shop or restaurant washroom? There is a chart pasted on the door, that you can easily notice while sitting on the seat. Observe carefully next time, it has a bunch of tasks and cells, about the cleaning of the washroom or lavatory. And everytime there's cleaning done, you draw a swoosh against the relevant column.

It all boils down the approach of the founding members or the core team. If this swoosh is the attitude towards people issues or behavioral aspects of the business, rest assured you are heading for a major disaster.

What will work is an intervention dedicated towards creating Team Alignment and ensuring everybody is on the same page. A simple yet clear vision for all will work wonders in the long run. Productivity and performance will be a natural outcome.

The Why of what we are doing is essential to human beings and acts as a driving force.

VIII

What constitutes a team

The Cambridge dictionary defines a Team as, 'a group of people who act together to achieve something.'

So what exactly is a team essentially? A Team is a group of people working together to achieve a common goal. When you put this in the context of a business what you get is an organizational structure with a set hierarchy in place. Everybody has a job role, a well defined KRA and the KPIs to achieve their individual targets.

It is easy to get lost in the complex jungle and start operating as an individual identity operating from an island cut off from the rest of the society. In fact this is precisely the experience a lot of employees report experiencing in their daily lives. There's either too much supervision and micromanagement or none at all.

The formulation of a team is preceded by the creation of a game. Before getting on to teams and performance consider going back to the basic idea of a game and how the game then brings forth the necessity to have a team in place.

What is a game? A game is a set of predefined actions with a definite goal that suggests achievement or victory or success.

Let's take the analogy of Cricket. What defines success is whoever has scored more runs at the end of the game. That's the winner.

Then there are KRAs and KPIs. A batsman, a bowler, a fielder, a wicketkeeper, a captain, and an umpire. Each of these roles have a set of well defined actions, that when done correctly lead to success.

A game also has rules. You cannot play cricket with a hockey stick and vice versa. You cannot come to the office wearing beachwear or attend an Indian wedding in a Christian gown, or eat pork or beef on certain occasions.

Not following the rules, breaking the rules or manipulating would result in you being unproductive or losing out on the opportunity to win or succeed.

This is precisely how a business operates. You need to have the game charted out clearly and rules in place for everybody to follow. Now, you are talking about the team and performance.

Notice, every person on the team has a different personality, no two players act the same way, there is uniqueness to every person. This difference in the style of functioning is what creates friction or clashes. Because like everything else human beings bring to the table their own sense of individuality.

There are teams that do exceedingly well and there are teams that don't. Some teams seem to have cracked the code and achieved massive success. While some teams struggle for survival. Why this glaring difference? There's obviously an X factor at play that distinguishes the great teams from the good or mediocre or poor teams. What is the X factor?

That elixir is Team Alignment. There are teams that operate with members completely in sync with each other and over achieve their targets. Outside the purview of business in the armed forces or sports there are teams that dominate for decades.

People often confuse alignment with agreement, in fact they collapse the two, as if they are one, though they actually aren't. Quite the contrary happens when people agree on something. You have riots and violence when people agree that what they believe and agree upon jointly is God's word. It isn't. Therefore, agreement isn't alignment. What is alignment? Look at the graphic below:

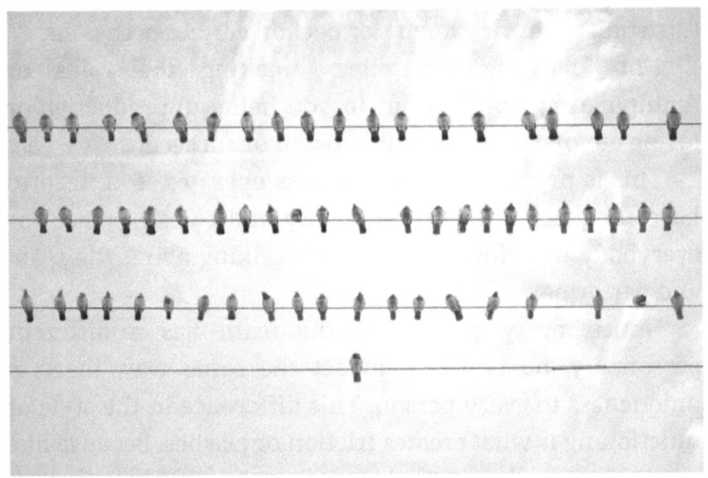

Alientation

'This is what agreement really does. Isolates and alienates people.'

This is alignment:

Victory

'You and I are different, I may not agree with you on everything, but we will get aligned so we win.' This is alignment.

Alignment is combining one's efforts and actions with another consistent with the rules of the game, such that the team wins as an outcome. The differences, or opinions don't matter. They cease to exist in the moment where you are aligned and acting as a team to win the game. Read this a couple of times, let it sink.

Alignment is accepting the differences and agreeing to combine the efforts to ensure victory. Period.

IX

COVID-19 and the tectonic shift in team and performance management

In the world of diplomacy and international relations there's the pre and post 9/11. Likewise in the domain of business there'll always be pre and post Covid. Business as we knew it was transformed forever, albeit by a crucible.

There is no doubt that technology has impacted and altered our way of life. What would have otherwise been 10-20 years of time frame to penetrate deep in the hinterlands of India, happened in less than 2 years.

The popularity of Amazon and Flipkart was limited to the metros. From nice to have it went to a must have during the lockdown. Everybody from a farmer, to a village lad to a homemaker suddenly was forced to get accustomed to using technology, it wasn't an option.

Look around and you will find the veggies and fruit sellers using PayTm. GPay is used by auto drivers and small mom and pop convenience stores alike. Apart from the well lauded and publicized government efforts to popularize UPI and QR codes, the pandemic was a natural catalyst.

This dramatically changes the way we conduct ourselves as business owners and professionals. We no longer have the convenience or rather the inconvenience of having every meeting in person. We do miss the camaraderie and banter of a tete-a-tete do doubt, but for someone living in Bangalore and Mumbai, having a Zoom meet is boon not bane. You save a lot of money and precious time that can now be allocated to more fruitful chores.

As the world returns to normalcy and back to office is loud, silently but consistently people prefer working from the comfort of their homes. A lot of corporate employees, managers and techies are openly voicing their displeasure at having to work from the office as a mandate rather than choice.

Internationally an increasing number of businesses are choosing to go remote full time. As a business it is a major cost saving exercise and mind you a lot of companies thrived and did phenomenally well despite the team working remote and no personal contact.

This also changes how we look at teams, members, their dynamics and communication with managers and bosses.

Presentations and client meetings need to be managed efficiently in a world that operates remotely. As a worker the skills to learn powerpoint, tech setup for Zoom or video conferencing, body language and expressions for an online meet are critical.

In a workplace setting where you cannot monitor people in person, you are not sitting directly in front of them and cannot obviously hover on their head all day, it takes a very different set of skills to be an effective manager. So it's not just the worker who must upskill or unlearn and relearn, it's also the team manager who must be willing to acquire new wings.

What has dramatically shifted is the use of tools and apps available with the use of technology. So you have a Darwin Box or Gray the HR for attendance and payroll management, to internal communication apps like Slack or Trello. There are now actually a whole range of companies that exist that mainly cater to other businesses that operate remotely.

If you look at this from the perspective of the founder or senior management like the CEO, this allows a lot more flexibility and freedom in terms of their own location. You could be living in Canada and manage a business in India remotely.

The best part is the MIS activity is completely out of the way. You longer have to ask the field team to report, and collate and submit it to the director, and then he would report to his VP, etc. This is obsolete stuff now. With the entire business including the CRM on the cloud platform with Salesforce, Zoho, Freshworks and others, at the click of a button you can actually monitor the complete operations, analyze and get the reports without having to ask anybody.

If you are the key decision maker in the business, this does something magical for you. See usually the staff or lower rung knows what's beingmonitored or scored, because you are asking for it. Now, one day you could be looking at all the calls made, the next payments collected and customer experience on the third. What this does is as a founder or stakeholder you are no longer dependent on the team leaders to actually provide you with vital information. You can quietly sip your Tequila from the Bahamas, listen to how customer complaints are being handled. I mean, this gives you an insane amount of freedom doesn't it? Same is true for product based companies as well.

If you are a first generation entrepreneur or have been handed the family mantle, you no longer need to limit your growth, simply for the sake of control. Here's what traditionally happens in family owned businesses. The first generation struggles and builds, the next manages that and tries to survive. Here's the problem with this solution, the marketplace is so dynamic today, you would be out of business in a jiffy, and won't even know it.

Look around, how many businesses do you know that are in the range of 50-100 Crores for the last 30 years. Effectively you are only managing and surviving the business and avoiding competing with the new players for the fear of failure, which in effect is suicidal. They will get you. Nobody, I repeat, no enterprise is indispensable. Everything is a matter of time and technology. Somebody out there is building something to move your cheese, whether you like it or not, believe it or not, know it or not, want it or not. The whole idea is to grow beyond what you know or think is possible. How do you do that? By building extraordinary teams.

How do you do that? By allowing people in the business to own a stake, be the shareholders of your business. When people you work with and partner with operate from a sense of ownership, not a penny or paperclip gets wasted. I kid you not.

There is a book I strongly recommend you read, if you already haven't. The Three Laws of Performance written by Steve Zaffron and Dave Logan. Whatever it is that I have laid out before you today, there is a relevant precedent in the business history of the world and companies have caused magical transformation by applying simple techniques that bring forth ownership in the team. Ownership is the highest form of responsibility. It's like being a parent. A mother doesn't need a reminder to feed the baby, she does that as a matter of her fullest natural self expression. A mother is who she is and is clear and settled about it.

With this I rest my case. Said briefly be willing to unlearn and relearn, be emotionally intelligent and build extraordinary teams.

Bibliography

- Amazon https://www.smartinsights.com/digital-marketingstrategy/

  online-business-revenue-models/amazon-casestudy/

- Bill Gates https://youtu.be/zPx5N6Lh3sw

- http://psychology.iresearchnet.com/sports-psychology/

  bodyimage-and-self-esteem/self-appraisal-in-sport/

- https://youtu.be/SwQhKFMxmDYChapters (Dr. Andrew Huberman)

- https://youtu.be/RKK7wGAYP6k (Lera Boroditsky)

- https://en.wiktionary.org/wiki/monkey_trap

- https://www.devdiscourse.com/article/entertainment

  /179192 0-children-should-get-property-Only-after-parents-deathvijaypat-singhania

- https://tech.hindustantimes.com/amp/tech/news/

  tinder-swindler-banned-from-online-dating-App-find-out-how-hepreyed-on-women-71644471907847.html

- https://www.google.com/

url?sa=t&source=web&rct=j&url=

- https://scholar.harvard.edu/files/jenniferlerner/

  files/
annual_review_manuscript_june_16_final.final_.pdf
  &ved=2ahUKEw
ijg5r12b3AhWilYBHZehQFnoECBIQAQ
  &usg=AOvVaw19sQExxg WL9iFDsqMX0wsD

- http://www.wernererhard.com/
  https://www.ncbi.nlm.nih.gov/pmc/articles/
  PMC6926721/

- https://chuckgarcia.com/2018/04/25/emotional-intelligencecase-study-elon-musk-of-tesla-inc/

- Roberto Benigni, Life is beautiful (Movie), 1997

- Steve Jobs https://youtu.be/UF8uR6Z6KLc

- Steve Zaffron & Dave Logan, The Three Laws of Performance (2011)

- Veda Vyasa, Bhagavad Gita, Sanskrit, 1ST Millennium BCE

- Viktor Frankl, Man's search for meaning, Beacon Press (English), 1946

- Zara https://www.tradegecko.com/blog/zara-supply-chainits-secret-to-retail-success 13

Meet The Author

Parashar Pandya

Parashar is a Career Salesman with over 2 decades of business development experience across sectors viz. Logistics, Garment manufacturing & Exports, L&D & Education. He is passionate about linguistics, communication & emotional intelligence. Parashar loves to travels & lives in Mumbai. Connect with him on Twitter/ PandyaParashar or email parasharbpandya@gmail.com

Printed by Libri Plureos GmbH in Hamburg, Germany